Roses in the Snow:

How I Survived After My Wife Died from Cancer

A Diary through Grief

DAVID C. MCCLELLAN

DAVID C. MCCLELLAN

Copyright © 2018 David C. McClellan

ISBN: 978-1722021771

ISBN-13: 978-1720819745

Cover photo: by Emma Dermott

via Flickr Creative Commons
https://www.flickr.com/photos/7819319@N05/2391379451/in/
photolist-4DjrNc-Ck9Knz-bJSCLp-MvjQiW-rFQLAt-qK4bRX-RcdGkm-
rpoaEZ-auMwdf-9Ade8H-F5LY7-4scH2c-rFKp5D-n9rK2Z-
rDyuM9-64oSDy-zBNZL-aERegN-e99VjB-Sf521Y-n9ttFf-
e87qYi-91o3oB-oauBL1-84F3hM-qrjJe-dwieVz-64oSFh-rK4ymV-
rGLUC3-rLxFJp-Qestuf-fDJrUQ-fD4LCT-bNcBH2-rFQKFx-rJX1qH-
rr7y8e-rGAb3D-rJoE2G-qPhJ23-rpXSig-rF2mcy-rJRqUG-rHzpBT-
rK5Q8n-rsnYQJ-rr3yx1-qPTKCP-rJmDUw

INTRODUCTION

It was New Year's Eve, 1972. I had just turned 16 and was still learning how to drive. The skating rink was in walking distance, though, and it was hosting an all-night-skate party.

My brother and I laced up and burned off some energy. After a while, the DJ announced that the next song would be a "Ladies' Choice" skate. Ugh. I had been here for these before, and usually, a fourth-grader would ask me to skate. I hid in the men's room.

I had discovered the beautiful creatures called girls a few years earlier, but was still very shy and awkward around them. I had never had a date. I'd asked a few girls to go to high school dances, only to be turned down.

When I poked my head out of the restroom, I saw my brother. Skating. With an angel. Blond hair, blue eyes -- my dream girl. Suddenly, I was no longer shy.

I skated over and informed the girl that she was skating with the wrong brother. Her name was Marie. We skated together the rest of the night. I told her that I'd one day ask her to marry me, just as my father had asked my mother to marry him on their first date. When you meet the one you are meant to be with, you just know it.

I was a junior at Whitehall High School. She was a freshman at our rival, Northampton High. We were both wearing bell bottoms -- hers high-waisted, mine low-slung hip huggers. The first song we skated to was "For The Good Times" by Ray Price.

As it was New Year's Eve, we kissed. Then, we exchanged numbers. I got a girl's phone number! My brother wasn't upset -- she wasn't really his type.

For whatever reason, I waited four days to call her. Her sister later told me that Marie spent those four days staring at the phone.

Forty-two years later, in the summer of 2014, Marie started talking about life insurance. She said, "I'm going to die before you. You need to increase my life insurance."

I was supposed to go first. All of her relatives had lived into their 80s and 90s. All of mine had died in their 40s, 50s, and 60s.

We looked at the cost of increasing her policy and figured that we would be better off putting extra money into savings. I really could not conceive of Marie dying before me. We agreed to stash an extra $20 a month into our savings account. Want to make God laugh? Make plans.

Three months later, she was gone. She was only 56.

Much of what you read in this book, I wrote with tears streaming down my face. I was lost, alone, and in pain. I began posting on Facebook -- poems, prayers, promises. Family, friends, and acquaintances offered me support. Many suggested that I write a book. Me? Write a book? Ridiculous. I spent 30 years working in lumber yards.

But then, some comments I received made it clear that I was not the only one finding comfort in my musings. So I committed to a year of chronicling my grief and yes, my healing. I later gathered those posts, added in some of the back story, and am presenting it here in hopes that this book will help someone going through a similar, heartbreaking loss.

About that title… I spent most of my life in eastern Pennsylvania, where winter can be unpredictable. Some years, the only snow is on TV. Other years are brutal, with six months of snow cover. Near the end of one of those harsh ones, it began to warm. Snow melted and roses bloomed. Then, just when we thought spring had arrived, again it snowed. Yet there, poking through the snow, was the rose and its promise of new life.

My journey through grief has been like that: painful loss, then signs of new life and happiness, then grief returning in waves. It's been years now, and I still think about Marie every day. My sadness, though, as powerful as it was, could not stop the snow from melting. It could not stop the robins and bunnies from appearing. It could not stop the roses from blooming anew.

If you are hurting, grieving some terrible loss, I hope the following pages will help you see those roses in the snow. I promise you, they will come.

-- Dave McClellan, 2018

PART ONE: SUMMER

Being a substitute teacher, I was on summer vacation the first day of August, 2014. Our motorhome needed new brakes. So I drove to the RV repair shop, bringing a book to read while I waited.

We are a Penn State family. I had season tickets to Penn State football for many years. It was a three-hour drive from our house to Penn State. After some initial reluctance (and a little begging on my part) Marie agreed and we bought a trailer.

The trailer was nice, but it was not practical for Penn State weekends. RV parking at Penn State is in a large open field with no utilities. I told Marie we needed a motorhome. We traded the trailer for a Class A motorhome -- one of the big rigs that look like busses. She never liked that rig and when a tire blew out on the way home from camping, she told me to trade it for something newer and smaller. So we traded it for a Class C motorhome with a sleeping area over the cab.

We used the camper for several Penn State weekends and for three camping weekends a year with our church group, where or ten or 12 families would meet at an RV campground. Marie always grumbled about camping -- the rain, the bugs, the long drive -- but we worked out a deal: I'd set up, cook, and clean. She was to sit, relax, and let me get her drinks. Then, she would smile.

About two hours into the RV repairs, Marie called asking how long I would be.

She had been driving to her job -- as Director of Operations at a company that designed and produced blister packaging for medical equipment -- but started seeing double, so turned around and went home. I was stuck, miles away, unable to get to her. Looking back, that was a good analogy for the next few months: I was nearby but completely helpless.

I told her I would be home as soon as the repairs were done. It ended up taking eight hours. It was a Friday, and we decided to see if the problem cleared up with a weekend of rest.

I'm sure that weekend was filled with mundane chores and some TV. I am sure Marie was concerned about her vision, but neither of us was in panic mode. We probably attended church on Sunday, as was our habit. But that Monday was one of the worst days of my life.

Marie's vision had not cleared up. I drove her to a local emergicenter to see a doctor. After running a few tests, he urged us to go to the nearest hospital. I was beginning to think it might be serious; however, being an optimist, I was not worried.

At the hospital, they did tests, scans, and x-rays. After several hours, a physician's assistant came to speak to us.

She said, "You have metastatic cancer. We can't help you here. We're going to transfer you to the main hospital. My shift is over, so good luck."

The cancer was a melanoma that started in her digestive tract and had already spread to her bones and several organs.

We, of course, were stunned. Numb. Neither of us cried. Neither talked for quite some time, as we were both trying to process the information.

I began to feel faint. I asked the nurse if I could lie down. Immediately, they put me on a stretcher and attached various monitors. I told them I did not need or want the attention, but they admitted me.

Marie was tougher.

She always had been. She was a way better athlete than I was. She was a twirler in her high school band and even as an adult would pick up a baton and go through a routine. She played second base on her neighborhood softball team.

But she had always refused to seek medical attention for physical problems. If I am not feeling well, I go to a doctor. Sinus infection, I take antibiotics. Poison ivy, get a shot in the butt. Knee problems, have ACL replacement surgery. Her response to each of these was the same: tough it out.

She also suffered from depression, often struggling to get through the day. She tried medication for a short while, but stopped as she did not like the side effects -- feeling dopey and not in control. I begged her for years to try a different medication. She refused. I told her there was no shame in correcting a chemical imbalance. She did not want to hear it. She went to a counselor and simply toughed it out.

But I did not realize the extent of her toughness until her battle with cancer.

A few months before her diagnosis, she had fallen and injured her back. She complained of pain for weeks, yet would not go to a doctor. One of the tests used during her diagnosis was a chest X-ray. As the doctor looked at the film, he asked when Marie had broken her shoulder.

I will always wonder if things would have been different. If we would have caught the cancer in an earlier stage... If she had gone to the doctor the day she fell… If, if, if …

I resolved that we were in for a winnable fight. She saw it differently.

One of the first things she said to me was, "Find someone new."

This was typical of Marie: thinking of others before herself. She knew I was not meant to be alone and was concerned about leaving me. I told her I would wait awhile, as we were going to beat this cancer.

After the diagnosis, I called my daughter, Kristy, who was 33 and living with her husband Lucas in St. John, New Brunswick, Canada. She worked as a consultant for an insurance company and did a great deal of traveling.

Me: "Kristy, your mom has cancer."

Kristy: "Fuck."

I called my son, Brad, a 25-year-old bartender living in State College, Pennsylvania.

Me: "Brad, your mom has cancer."

Brad: "Fuck."

I agree. Cancer. Fuck.

I did my best to convince them that they should not worry, and everything would be fine. We'll beat this.

Neither of our kids inherited my optimism. Like their mom, they're worriers. Both offered to come home. I told them to live their lives; I would keep them posted and call if I needed them. Neither of them listened. They both tied up things at their jobs and headed home.

Thank God. I needed them both more than I knew. Yes, I literally thank God. I believe He moved them against my protestations. He knew my needs better than I did.

This was my Facebook post on August 6, 2014:
> Marie is in the hospital. We know she has cancer. In order to treat it, doctors have to determine the type and location of the cancer. Test after test after test.

Most of us grew up watching countless TV shows about doctors and hospitals. Many of them were hour-long dramas. A patient would show up with puzzling symptoms. Doctors ran tests, conferred with other doctors, and talked with the patient. A treatment plan was established. Medicine was delivered. The patient was cured.

"Oh, thank you doctor, you saved my life!"

"I'm just doing my job," said the humble doctor.

All this is accomplished in an hour. Real life is nothing like that. Real life is hours, days, and weeks of waiting and worrying. Real life is messy and uncertain.

Asking for prayers for my wife. Please don't ask for details. I will share more when it is appropriate.

August 14, 2014
Marie is home and resting. We go to see the specialist tomorrow to discuss treatment options. Thank you all for thoughts, prayers, food, etc. We both have good attitudes and strong faith and we are prepared for a bumpy ride. It's called life.

Our church has a group called Lovin' from the Oven. When they get word that someone is in need, they cook. For several days, people showed up with delicious meals in Tupperware. When there was no more room in the refrigerator, I asked them to slow down. God provided through good people. Thank you, St. John's United Church of Christ.

August 15, 2014
Okay, we know Marie has cancer. What are we going to do? Chemo, radiation, immunotherapy? Whatever it is, can we start? The waiting and doing nothing is driving me crazy.

I have always been an optimist. I think a belief that better times are coming helps get you through trying times. That is not to say I never get anxious or down sometimes. One year, when our kids were still young and Christmas was still a big deal, I got laid off three weeks before Christmas.

We had planned on getting a PlayStation game system for the kids. But since it was $100 that we did not have, we would have to deal with two disappointed kids. Christmas Eve, we went to my parents' house to exchange gifts with my family. My parents were doing okay and my gift from them was… $100! The price of a PlayStation. I conferenced with Marie and made a quick trip to the toy store. The kids were getting a PlayStation!

After a few hours, we headed home. When we pulled in to the drive, we noticed a package on the porch. It had a tag: "To Kristy and Brad, from Santa." It was a PlayStation.

Yes, Virginia, there is a Santa Claus! Marie and I were in tears at the anonymous generosity. In a matter of hours, we went from not being able to afford the game system to having two of them.

We later learned that our best friends played Santa. The good Lord will provide in abundance.

This optimism made me believe that Marie would beat the cancer. I remained optimistic (or blind to the facts?) throughout her ordeal. I think that may be why finally having to admit the battle was lost was so painful.

I had an interview several weeks ago that I thought went well. When they chose another candidate, I was upset and started to get down on myself. With my family's current situation, it would not be possible for me to begin a new, full-time teaching job now.

I prayed and asked God to get me the job.

He answered, "I need you somewhere else."

I am learning that, while I am in the car, I am not driving. I have taken my hands off the wheel and turned the driving over to God. The Bible says that you have to become like a child in order to enter Heaven. I used to think that meant to turn from sin and become innocent like a child. Maturity, and Bible study, changed my mind.

No child is innocent. We are all born into sin. Think about a child. He loves his parents without restraint. He depends upon them to meet all of his needs. He trusts them completely. It is only when we approach God as a child approaches a parent -- completely loving, dependent, and trusting -- that we can truly feel His love.

Marie grew up in a Catholic family. We were married in a Catholic church. She attended Catholic church and both our children were baptized and confirmed in a Catholic church. Though I tried, I never felt at home or comfortable in her church. I stopped going.

Sometime in my early 40s, I felt like I was adrift, there was something missing in my life. I started attending a UCC church with my brother and my friends. It was led by an amazing pastor. He was extremely intelligent and consistently delivered powerful, thought-provoking sermons. I started going regularly.

Marie felt that we should worship as a family, so we brought Brad. Kristy was in college at this point and rarely joined us.

I taught Sunday School and Brad participated in many youth events. Every summer, we'd go on mission trips to places that had suffered storm damage or needed a little help. For a week, the adults would teach the teens how to use power tools, pound nails, or paint. We would improve someone's living situation and in the process, share our faith with them.

Before I did this, I could not understand how a person could give up a week of vacation to work. Now that I have done it, I know that those weeks were the most rewarding times of my life. The feeling you get when you get to know someone while giving of yourself is incredible. Once you do it, you want to do it again and again. Our mission trip leader, Marge, coined the term "being bitten by the heart bug."

<u>August 22, 2014</u>
I called the doctor to find out what treatment plan he had in mind and when it would start. He told me they had a plan but were waiting to find out if the drug company would pay for it. If I could reach through the phone, there would be a dead doctor.

The drug company ultimately did agree to pay for it, as it was a brand new treatment option and they were still gathering data. Otherwise, it would have cost a couple hundred thousand dollars. Don't get me wrong. If that had been the case, we would have borrowed the money, even if it meant being in debt the rest of our lives.

Marie hated to spend money and preferred small, inexpensive jewelry over big, gaudy, expensive stuff. We worked hard for our money and she was always reluctant to part with it. I can be frugal but thanks to her, we never carried credit card debt and were able to build a decent retirement fund.

<u>August 28, 2014</u>
My wife's treatments begin tomorrow. We are remaining cautiously optimistic.

Worry. Marie was a champion at worrying. If we planned an outdoor party, "What if it rains?" If we planned a trip, "What if Brad gets sick?" or "How will we pay for that?" "What if lightning strikes our house?"

Marie firmly believed that if something could go wrong, it would. She didn't invent worrying; she came from a family of worriers. Most of the females in her family spent their time imagining catastrophic events that might occur.

Whenever one of our camping trips approached, the grumbling began. Marie would say, "I'm not going! It's going to rain. It will be too hot, etc." She'd ultimately go along, while telling me how much she hated camping. But we had a deal: If she'd go camping, I'd set up, cook, and clean. She was to sit and let me get her drinks. Then, she would relax and smile.

I never worry. I believe worry is an insult to God. I deal with what is, not with what might happen. She worried too much. I will admit, at times, her worry led us to take precautions or make backup plans. I am not going to start worrying; however, I may start thinking more about the consequences of my actions.

September 1, 2014

Marie still has double vision which makes everything difficult for her. She can't drive and has trouble concentrating.

We went to an opthamologist who measured her for special glasses. They came up with a huge lens that looked like a one-inch-thick prism. We ordered them. By the time the glasses came in, Marie was bedridden and on pain medication. She no longer needed them. We never picked them up.

September 11, 2014

This is a poem I wrote a short while after 9/11:

Never Forget!
There's a crack in the mirror, one that lets the tears show through.
The world's turned upside down. I don't know what to do.
The marketplace has crumbled in a heap of smoking ash,
In New York City, the capital of cash.
Children look for answers; parents have none to give.
It's been said "Why can't we live and let live?"
We don't know why you hate us so.
This much I can tell you though.
You have awakened a mighty power.
And, while we don't know the day or the hour,
You will see this on our sail:
We will not tire,
We will not falter,
AND WE WILL NOT FAIL!

I know this poem does not have anything to do with Marie. It is related to grief. Thousands died that day. Countless families were grieving lost relatives. We as a nation, were grieving for lost souls and for a loss of innocence.

This was the first time I expressed my feelings in poetry. Like every good person alive and aware on 9/11/2001, I had been angry, confused, and afraid. I had so many emotions roiling inside me, I had to let them out. Poetry provided a way to vent. During Marie's illness and after her death, I would turn to poetry again.

PART TWO: AUTUMN

This is Marie's high school picture. It is easy to see how I fell in love at first sight.

I was the middle child of five, born in Pittsburgh to Sarah and Clair McClellan. My dad was very bright and creative. He chafed at working for people with less intelligence. He would quit or be fired from a job and we would pack up and move.

When we settled in Whitehall, my mom told him we were done moving. She got a job teaching home economics while he learned how to reupholster furniture and ran a business doing that out of our home.

Because we moved so many times, I was always "the new kid." The fact that I was small and wore glasses made me more of a target for bullies. I took my share of getting knocked down. But bullies soon learned that if they fought with me, I would find a way to hurt them. My father told me there is no such thing as a fair fight -- bite, kick, scratch, do whatever you have to do to make an enemy not want to fight you again. I'm not bragging, but several of my opponents have scars to remind them of the day we fought. Fortunately, I learned to use humor to deflect bullying, and my fighting days ended.

Marie was the fourth and youngest child born to Joseph and Mary Remsing -- the baby in a strict Catholic family. She had two sisters and a brother. Her oldest sister took her vows and became a nun when Marie was a toddler. One of her uncles was a priest. Needles to say, she grew up Catholic.

As a boy, I'd heard the story of how my father, on the first date with my mother, told her they would marry one day. History repeated itself when I met Marie. On first sight, I knew we were meant to be together.

We dated through high school. She introduced me to large family gatherings and foods I had never eaten before like cabbage and noodles, sauerkraut with brown sugar, and cucumber salad.

While her two sisters attended Catholic school, Marie and her brother attended public schools. Marie and her family lived in the house where her father was born. I had moved a lot, while Marie was entrenched. This may explain why Marie hated change and I embraced it.

Of course, the youngest child always enjoys more freedom than the first or second child. We heard, "I was never allowed to do that!" from her older sisters many times.

As teens, we once took an unescorted trip to Wildwood, NJ. I can hear her sisters now: "I was never allowed to do that!"

She joined my family on a vacation in Canada. "I was never allowed to do that!"

Three days after high school graduation, I headed off for Penn State, age 17. Marie, then still in high school, would drive up to spend weekends with me. "I was never allowed to do that!"

But this was always said with humor, never bitterness. Even before we were married, I was treated as a member of the family.

Marie and I never dated anyone else. While in college, I considered breaking up, thinking that maybe the grass was greener somewhere else. I didn't do it because I couldn't bear hurting her. We were meant to be together.

In my senior year, Marie bought a college class ring for me. We went to the jewelry store to pick it up. While there, I led her over to the engagement rings, pointed at one and said, "Do you like this one?" She exclaimed happily that she loved it. I made it official when we went back to my fraternity house and got down on one knee. A few weeks later, one of her sisters reminded me that I had not asked Marie's father for his permission/blessings. I promptly corrected that faux pas, and he approved.

At school, I had no direction other than to get a degree. I took every liberty and cut many classes. My parents were footing the bill and I did not realize the value of a college education. When I told my mom I might need an extra semester to graduate, she said I could take as many as I was willing to pay for. I doubled up my credit load in my last semester, worked like a dog, and graduated by the skin of my teeth. When the dean handed me my diploma, I said, "Are you sure?" Those four years went incredibly fast.

Four months after college graduation, we were married. My college fraternity brothers attended and were the hit of the party. As we left the reception, they all sang "Happy Trails" to us. To this day, our reception was one of the best parties I ever attended. Now it was time to find a job.

We moved to Asbury Park, New Jersey, where I took the first position I was offered: management trainee at 84 Lumber. Marie found work as a bookkeeper/secretary at a roofing company. We lived in a one-bedroom apartment, five blocks from the ocean. We were both very young and I was still very immature. I spent way too much time in bars while she spent way too much time sitting home alone. Looking back, I was very selfish. If I could, I would go back and do that part of our life together over.

I worked there two years to the day and knew it was time to move on. For the next 30 years, I worked for several different building material suppliers. I drove trucks and forklifts. I did retail inside sales and outside sales, calling on lumber yards as a wholesaler.

My career kind of mirrored my dad's. In almost every job, I felt I was more intelligent than my boss. Whether that's true or not is open to debate. Regardless, I quit or was fired from too many jobs. Marie spent decades at each of her jobs, but I changed employers about every two years.

My last job in the industry was managing a millwork company that supplied local builders. I realized that I had spent enough time in an unrewarding industry. About that same time, I started teaching Sunday school. I loved it, and the kids loved me. Several people said I should become a teacher. I finally listened and at 53, I went back to school to earn my masters degree in education. This time, I was paying for my own education and took it much more seriously.

I graduated in three years with honors. Marie was very supportive of me and was so proud when I graduated. I worked as a substitute, trying to find my own classroom. I was still doing that when Marie died.

Marie earned her associates degree in accounting from our local community college in 1978. Our marriage ended her education. Like every married couple, we had our ups and downs, our petty squabbles and our huge blow-ups. We always found a way to work through the tough times though. Any good mariage takes two people working hard for the same goals.

She worked in several different jobs through our years together. She always gave her all and was always loyal to her employer. She worked for a caterer for several years. I don't know the details, but her employer ran into financial problems and stopped paying her. She continued to show up and do her job anyway, believing the finances would improve and they would make things right. That's how loyal she was.

As Marie was handling our finances, she concealed the facts from me. I found out after she had gone six weeks without a paycheck. I insisted she give an ultimatum to her employer -- that he make up all back pay before she returned to work. There was no money, so she left the job.

Marie's next job was as a secretary/bookkeeper for a small company dealing in plastics. One of the owners was a high school classmate. When he left to start his own company, she went with him. The company started with five people working in a space above a garage.

Over the years, the company grew, and Marie assumed more and more responsibilities. A few years before her illness, the company had grown to several locations with hundreds of employees. Marie was promoted to a director of the company. This promotion and commensurate pay raise allowed me to make my career change.

It was much more than a job to Marie. Her coworkers were her extended family. When she was diagnosed, I offered to take her anywhere in the world. We would do whatever she wanted to do. Her response? "I want to work." As she could not drive, I would take her to work and then pick her up when she was tired. In October, she was no longer able to work.

Two years after Marie passed away, her classmate sold his company. He then distributed over a million dollars to his employees who built the company. He sent me a letter explaining the situation and thanking me for Marie's service. Included in the letter was a check.

I received two lessons from this. The first lesson is: there are still good people in the world. This occurred as I was contemplating retirement and worrying if I had enough money put away to make it work. The second lesson was that I should not worry over money. If I put my trust in God, I may not get what I want -- but I will get what I need.

Check out my favorite Bible verse, Matthew 6:24-34:

> No one can serve two masters; for either he will hate the one and love the other, or else he will be loyal to the one and despise the other. You cannot serve God and mammon.

> Therefore I say to you, do not worry about your life, what you will eat or what you will drink; nor about your body, what you will put on. Is not life more than food and the body more than clothing?

> Look at the birds of the air, for they neither sow nor reap nor gather into barns; yet your heavenly Father feeds them. Are you not of more value than they? Which of you by worrying can add one cubit to his stature?

So why do you worry about clothing? Consider the lilies of the field, how they grow: they neither toil nor spin; and yet I say to you that even Solomon in all his glory was not arrayed like one of these. Now if God so clothes the grass of the field, which today is, and tomorrow is thrown into the oven, will He not much more clothe you, O you of little faith? Therefore do not worry, saying, 'What shall we eat?' or 'What shall we drink?' or 'What shall we wear?'

For after all these things the Gentiles seek. For your heavenly Father knows that you need all these things. But seek first the kingdom of God and His righteousness, and all these things shall be added to you. Therefore do not worry about tomorrow, for tomorrow will worry about its own things. Sufficient for the day is its own trouble...

As I listened to a song on the radio, I realized that John Denver echoed these sentiments in his song "Sweet Surrender": Sweet, sweet surrender/ Live, live without care/ Like a fish in the water, like a bird in the air.

Surrender to God. Put your trust in Him. Fish and birds do not worry where their next meal is coming from; God provides. I have found that when I surrendered, took my hands off the wheel, and trusted God, things fell into place. I still have my struggles and sad times. but I remain hopeful of a better tomorrow.

October 10, 2014
We get to meet two new doctors today. Yay!

As we journeyed through the medical system, amazing, overworked nurses did their best to keep Marie comfortable and keep us both positive. On a rare occasion, a doctor popped in, uttered a few words, and disappeared. Through the entire process, only one doctor sat down with us. I was unimpressed at best, and a little pissed off at worst, at the other healthcare practitioners we met.

October 13, 2014
I spent an hour and a half building a wheelchair ramp.
We are now handicap-accessible!

My years of working in lumber yards paid off. The ramp allowed us to get Marie in and out of the house while in her wheelchair.

October 14, 2014
And… She's home! With oxygen and all kinds of new pills. Cancer sucks.

Cancer.

I was a sophomore in college when we lost my grandmother to cancer. She never drank or smoked.

My father fought prostate cancer for several years. He was 70 and I was 42 when he lost the battle. He quit smoking in his 20s and I saw him drink one beer in my lifetime.

Shortly after his death, my mom was diagnosed with colon cancer. She had surgery and beat it, though we are in the process of losing her to Alzheimer's. She never drank or smoked.

Marie and I had a German Shepherd/Border Collie mix dog named Simba. He was wicked smart and very loyal. He was ten when he got bone cancer and we had to put him down. It broke our hearts; he was the best dog ever. Simba, of course, never drank or smoked.

Marie was 54 when cancer attacked and took her from us. Marie had a drink on a rare occasion but never smoked. Cancer sucks.

October 15, 2014
Our son and daughter have both put their lives on hold to come home and help. I love them both and feel terrible about what they are going through.

"Ouch, Ouch, Ouch!"

"I sorry, I sorry, I sorry!" is what I remember from the birth of our daughter. After 20 hours of painful labor, the petite Chinese American doctor was using forceps to help the process along.

As Marie first held our baby, she looked at me and said, "We're not doing this again."

It was eight years before I convinced her to try again. The second pregnancy was much worse for Marie. She developed preeclampsia and was ordered by the doctor to rest. Always bull-headed and never one to like or listen to doctors, she soldiered on. She kept working until a doctor ordered her hospitalized and put on bed rest.

Kristy stayed with relatives as I stayed next to Marie's bed. The waiting was on. At one point, our friends said I needed a break and invited me to dinner. Marie told me to go. Shortly after I left, my mom stopped in to visit Marie. As I was enjoying my dinner, socializing with friends, Marie had a seizure and went into convulsions. The baby was killing her.

Doctors were paged and were seen running from the cafeteria to get to her. Brad was delivered by C-section and crisis was averted. When I finished eating, I called to see how Marie was doing. My mom answered the phone and suggested I might want to come and meet my son.

He was a month early and very small. We had to feed him formula with a one-ounce bottle. It took him an hour to drink it. Marie was delusional. She claimed there were spiders on the wall. She believed there was a projector in the room across the hall and that the hospital workers were trying to torture her and make her crazy. I feared that she would not recover her senses. I felt like I had gained a son and lost my wife.

She stayed in the hospital for a week. Though she recovered, after this experience, her depression worsened. We had a boy and a girl and decided it was best to stop there.

When I commented to people later how I'd felt bad about not being there for Marie when Brad was born, people suggested that God had shielded me from seeing Marie in distress.

October 17, 2014
Warning
Gray clouds in the morning
I should have seen the warning
I was walking along
Singing a song
Enjoying my life
Without any strife
When out of nowhere
Comes a really bad scare
Why did she get cancer
No one has an answer
They'll treat it
We'll beat it
Life will go on
We'll see a new dawn

October 24, 2014
Today I have no time for tears. Today, I will live, I will love, and I will laugh. In some tomorrow, down the road, there will be tears.

I used to think I was in control. With maturity comes an understanding that, sometimes, no matter what you do, things will happen. I used to think I was driving the car. I realize now I am a passenger. I still need to pay attention and do my part but I took my hands off the wheel years ago. Take me where you need me, Lord.

October 27, 2014
Sunrise, blue eyes. Starry skies, teary eyes. Pain and sorrow, hope for tomorrow. Love song, stay strong.

November 1, 2014
After several rounds of radiation and two immunotherapy treatments, Marie's symptoms seemed to be improving. We went to the doctor expecting to begin the third treatment.

The doctor quietly told us the treatments were not working -- that, in fact, the cancer was growing more rapidly. She advised hospice care. Marie wanted to continue the fight. It was time to face the cold, hard truth. We did not speak on the car ride home.

Driving to the hospital, Marie had been in very good spirits. Most of her symptoms had eased, and her vision improved. To us, it seemed the treatments were working. We are going to beat this thing and get on with our lives.

The doctor was not at the meeting. We rarely saw the lead doctor, as he was constantly traveling and lecturing about the amazing results his new therapy achieved. He had his assistant deliver the horrible news.

Yes, radiation had shrunk some of the tumors, providing the relief Marie experienced. But the other tumors were in fact growing even more rapidly, completely unresponsive to the immunotherapy drugs. (Chemotherapy was never even discussed as an option. We trusted the "world renowned expert" on this type of cancer.)

The doctor recommended we discontinue treatment and enter hospice and palliative care. The news was almost as shocking as the initial diagnosis. It was time to take off the rose-colored glasses and face reality.

I have not included any doctors' names. While I do not blame them for the ultimate outcome, I do feel Marie and I could have been treated better. One exception: Dr. Ric Baxter practices palliative care at a hospital in Bethlehem, Pennsylvania. He was sensitive to our situation and genuinely cares for each of his patients. He has an extremely comforting presence and was a welcome relief from the other doctors. He knew that travel was difficult for Marie, so he stopped what he was doing and drove to our house to explain hospice care.

<u>November 12, 2014</u>
Nah nah nah nah/ nah live for today
That's what the words in the rock song say
Come what may
Today is the day
You can't live in the past
Only the memories last
Trying to see tomorrow
Will only cause you sorrow
If you truly want to live
Today takes all you have to give
If you are ruled by your fears
You will waste away your years
Time should not be wasted
Life is meant to be tasted
Climb that mountain
Jump into that fountain
Kiss that girl
Dance in a whirl
Laugh out loud
Get lost in a crowd
Don't be in such a hurry
Don't spend a minute in worry
Stop being blue
Tell someone, "I love you!"

I walked into the falling snow to hide my falling tears.

My son, my daughter, and I spent the next weeks caring for Marie. Over a very short time, she lost the ability to walk. She became bedridden and was given larger and larger doses of stronger and stronger painkillers.

Marie's sister Jane came most days to help. She stopped eating. We knew her time was almost at an end.

I walked into our side yard as a light snow was falling. I just needed to breathe fresh air, to have time to myself, to cry.

Up until this point, I had tried to be optimistic and upbeat and keep everyone else's spirits up. They had put their lives on hold to help me care for Marie. That, and I guess it's a man thing not to let others see me cry.

<u>November 17, 2014</u>
My sister-in-law, Jane, had been coming to our house every day to assist in Marie's care. Tonight, she called to say she could not come tomorrow as her husband, my brother-in-law, passed away.

18

Jane's husband John had woken up and said he didn't feel well. Jane convinced him to go to the hospital. After several hours, he simply passed away. I'm not entirely sure of the cause. It was just his time. Jane had been a strength for me but now she had her own emergency. My heart was being ripped apart. We would comfort each other in the following months. I will always be grateful to her.

In my life, I have witnessed several different ways that people transition from Earthly to Eternal life. I was in eighth grade walking home from school on a cold, windy day. I felt the rush of wind when a pickup truck went by. Seconds later, I heard screeching tires and a thump. I looked up to see a body fall in front of the truck. A classmate and some friends had been caught doing mischief and were running across the road. Eddie was the last one in line, the body I saw fall.

One of my friend's mother had diabetes. I remember how she grew smaller over the last year of her life. First, they took her toes, then her foot, and finally both legs up to her knees. She died shortly after the last amputation.

I watched as one of Marie's grandmothers lost her mind to Alzheimer's. I saw the pain suffered by her family when she no longer recognized them. I watched as her other grandmother lost her physical abilities while remaining sharp mentally. They were both close to 90 years old when they passed.

I watched my father's battle with cancer and the seesaw ride of hope and despair.

A large group of our friends took a cruise to Bermuda. On that cruise, some of us took a side trip to go bell diving. The divers were to go in shifts. The first group suited up as we waited our turn. One older gentleman had suited up and was in the water on the ladder. He said, "I can't do this," then fell backwards into the water. They pulled him out, got him on deck, and gave him CPR. It was to no avail. Heart attack.

I was in my 20s when I lost a co-worker. A 17-year old had just gotten his pilot's license and was flying over a residential area, showing off his new skills. His skills weren't so good. As my young co-worker backed out of her driveway to go to work, the young pilot crashed into her car, killing them both.

That incident convinced me that when your time is up, your time is up. There is no point in worrying. Do you look up in the sky before you back out of your driveway?

I experienced the ups and downs of battling cancer with both my father and my wife. I gave up smoking, drink socially, on occasion, and try to keep my weight under control. Still, I know something is going to get me. I am hoping for a heart attack -- many years from now.

<u>November 18, 2014</u>
I met a beautiful girl when I was 16. She put up with me for the next 42 years (36 years of marriage). Today, I heard bells when she got her wings

As Marie slipped away in her final days, Kristy, Brad and I each took an hour here or there to get out of the house and breathe for a bit. I went to get a haircut. I was almost home and decided to turn around and pick up a few groceries. She passed away while I was in the store.

I don't believe she was afraid. I believe she knew she was dying even before we got the diagnosis. She had a very strong faith that there was something better on the other side. I think she wanted to be free of the pain.

When I recounted how I had not been there and felt terrible about it to friends, they said, "Maybe God was protecting you. Maybe he didn't want that to be your last memory of Marie." I have some smart friends.

Jane and John had joined Marie and I on a cruise to Bermuda shortly before Marie's diagnosis. Someone took a picture of our group. In the center were Marie and John. Little did we know they would both soon be gone.

While in Bermuda, we booked excursions. I agreed to go with Marie on a bus trip exploring the island. At the last minute, I changed my mind and went with my friends who rented scooters to explore the island on our own. Once again by being selfish, I robbed myself of time with Marie.

I can't change the past. I can learn from my mistakes. Very often, being selfish is extremely costly.

<u>November 19, 2014</u>
There will be a celebration of life memorial service for Marie on Saturday Nov. 22 at 3 pm at St. John's United Church of Christ on Broad St. in Nazareth, PA with a luncheon and time to reminisce following. All who knew and loved Marie are welcome.

One of Marie's co-workers gave a eulogy at her memorial service. He explained that one thing Marie loved was our camping trips. Everyone at work knew when a camping weekend was coming up. She would tell everyone. They were all sworn to secrecy: "Do not tell Dave how much I like camping!"

Truth be told, I was with her for 40 years. I knew that if she didn't like doing something, she wouldn't have done it. Our camping trips were the only times she truly relaxed and smiled.

November 20, 2014
Alone
The darkness of night
Used to mean peace
And pleasant dreams
Now I find no solace there
The weight of the world
Comes crashing down
I find myself
Alone
In a cold, dark place
The end of her pain
Was the beginning of mine
Faith tells me
She's in a better place
She's found her Heavenly home
And left me
Alone
Together for years
Lots of smiles
A few tears
Dave and Marie
Dave and Marie
Through thick and thin
Now it's just Dave
Alone
Where do I go from here
How will I find my way
Will I smile again
What will become of me
When will the pain ease
Why did she leave me
Alone

November 21, 2014
Yesterday's newspaper carried two obits, one for my wife and one for my brother-in-law. Note to God: Time out, please.

<u>November 22, 2014</u>

As a rule, funerals suck. Today we said goodbye to Marie in an amazing, uplifting ceremony which, except for the fact that it was about her, Marie would have loved. Thank you to all who have supported us in this difficult time. I met some amazing people and strengthened some existing friendships. Thank you, thank you, thank you!

When I was talking to the caterer, planning the funeral luncheon, she asked how many people we expected. I started counting family, close friends, and co-workers and came up with 25. After getting dubious looks, I refigured and said, 50? Still getting those looks, I said, "Let's go with 75." More than 120 people showed up to say goodbye.

It was a very positive experience. As I said, many more people showed up than we expected. We sang three songs. Two were hymns that Marie requested. The third, and last, was one her favorite songs, "Sweet Caroline."

This song is played at every Penn State football game and Marie loved to sing along with the crowd. Everyone at the memorial sang along, and then extended their condolences with smiles on their faces. Marie would have loved it.

All that being said, I'm not sure that was a good choice. Do you know how often "Sweet Caroline" comes on the radio? Did I mention that it is played at every Penn State game? For two years, every time I heard it, I stopped what I was doing and cried.

I have since mellowed and now, when I hear it, I smile at her memory. Maybe it was a good choice, after all.

<u>November 23, 2014</u>
I Will Never/Will I Ever
I will never
Hold her again
See her smile
Hear her laugh
Taste her cookies
Go camping with her
Kiss her lips
Hold her hand
Sit next to her in church
Eat dinner with her
Go down the shore with her
Buy presents for her

Decorate a Christmas tree with her
Celebrate Thanksgiving with her
Color Easter eggs with her
Stroke her hair
See her blue eyes
Point out deer to her in our backyard
Look at pictures of our kids together
Comfort her when she is sad
Take her to a movie
Take a walk with her
Will I ever
Smile again
See another sunny day
Love again
Laugh again
Live again?

These were obviously very dark days for me and my children. Not that I would ever consider suicide, but there were times when I questioned whether I wanted to go on alone. I believe thoughts like these come from the Evil One, who attacks us at our weakest moments. My faith and firm belief in God's love allowed me to quickly push these thoughts aside.

November 24, 2014
I wish it would leave
All I do is cry, cry
It hurts so bad
I wonder why, why
She said goodbye
They took her away, away
Gone forever
In the ocean she will sway, sway
Nothing more to say
My heart is broken, broken
Torn from my chest
No more words spoken, spoken
Her ring just a token
Cancer spoke her name, her name
That evil beast
Ever since it came, it came
Nothing is the same
If only I could take it out, take it out
Stomp on it
I would shout, shout

23

And shake it about
I would make it hurt, hurt
Rip it to pieces
Tear off its shirt, shirt
And cover it in dirt
I dry my eyes on my sleeve, my sleeve
Hurting so bad
I wish it would leave, just leave
So we would no longer grieve

I have had several surgeries. Each one involved recovery and rehab. Usually the rehab means physical therapy. The physical therapy can be strenuous and uncomfortable. You have a choice. You can work hard at therapy, deal with the effort and discomfort, or you can lie in your bed and complain about atrophied muscles. I've learned you have to pay the price. I have also learned that when you are going through a painful process, it seems to last forever.

Then, when you look back on painful times, it seems like they passed in the blink of an eye. Grief is much like that. You can sit in a corner and cry and never get over your loss or you can go through the steps of grieving and begin a new life.

Like they say, you can pay me now or you can pay me later. You have to go through the process. You will recover. Life does go on.

November 25, 2014
I can barely breathe. It is as if the world was sitting on my chest. I don't feel pain, I don't feel anything. Well, I do feel one thing: lost.

After many years together, we settled into our routines. Now she's gone and I am clueless as to how I am supposed to go on. I get out of bed because I am supposed to. I eat because I'm supposed to. I shower and shave because I'm supposed to. I go through mail and pay bills because I have to. Everything is an effort.

If I try to watch TV, nothing makes sense. Their mouths move. I hear voices, but I can't follow what they are saying. I am not working, because I could not possibly get through a day with a classroom full of kids.

My mind is just a jumble of what-ifs, whys, and what-nows. I really don't know when or if I will be ready to work again. I know I will have to at some point, because I am too young to retire.

I am going to start early. Thank you, God for family and friends who have supported me these last few months. I am thankful that Marie did not suffer. I am thankful for shelter from the storm. I am thankful for my church family and my faith, which makes my pain somewhat bearable. I am thankful for my career change, and even though I have not found a permanent position, I have faith that I will soon. To all my friends and family: Enjoy Thanksgiving and stay well.

Marie had grown up surrounded by her extended family. Her grandparents' farm had been parceled out in building lots for her aunts and uncles on her father's side. Two of her mother's sisters lived ten minutes away. All of this meant that birthdays and holidays were large family gatherings.

My family lived far from aunts, uncles and cousins, so our celebrations were small, intimate affairs. When Marie and I started dating, the large family gatherings were foreign and intimidating to me. Over time, as we lost grandparents, aunts, and uncles, the once-large raucous celebrations gave way to smaller, more somber gatherings. The joy of each occasion was clouded by remembrance of those no longer there.

PART THREE: WINTER

November 27, 2014
Thanksgiving is over. The kids are heading home, trying to restart
their lives. The hospital bed, wheelchair, and oxygen tanks have all
been returned. The room where Marie died is now empty, like my
heart. Part of me just wants to sit in that room to try to be with
her. The other part of me never wants to go in that room again.

Her parents gave us this land. We built this house. We put on
additions. We raised our children here. We celebrated holidays and
birthdays here. Now, it is a big, empty house. I'm not sure if it is
still my home.

November 28, 2014
Everyone else is shopping for Christmas. They are stringing lights
up outside. They are putting up trees and decorating their homes.
I am sitting on my couch and crying.

November 29, 2014
When you are married a long time, your conversations become
short.

"What do you want for dinner?"
"I don't care. Whatever."
"How was your day?"
"Okay."

Then you sit and wordlessly watch TV until you crawl into bed.
"Goodnight."
"Goodnight."

But there is someone there.
When they leave, everything changes. The house is bigger, the bed
is bigger. Or maybe you have become smaller.

Whichever it is, things are different. You are alone. Your friends
were there for you when she was sick. They were at the funeral.
Now, they have gone back to their lives. Now they are getting
ready for Christmas. Being alone sucks.

December 1, 2014
People say that Facebook is impersonal and that many "friends"
are not really friends. I can tell you that the birthday wishes I
received on Facebook today were a blessing, a light on a very dark
day. Thank you.

December 2, 2014
In the sweetness of life
No sorrow, no strife
We walk hand in hand
Through this bounteous land
All roads lead
To everything we need
She'll always be there
And about every care
She'll brush off with a shrug
And give me a hug
It will be alright
And we'll kiss goodnight
Knowing tomorrow
There will be no more sorrow
We will face all our fears
And cry no more tears
A gentle hand on my face
Will tell me she's in a better place
Though now I grieve
One day I will leave
Then I will see
She will be waiting for me.

December 3, 2014
Christmas is coming! Is that a happy pronouncement? Is it a
command to hurry because there is a deadline? Is it a sad
reminder that this will be your first Christmas without her?

Marie used to begin buying and wrapping presents in January. I
always waited until the last minute. Marie did all the inside
decorating, I was responsible for the outside light display.

The thought that Christmas is a celebration of God's love for us
does bring some peace to my troubled world. The thought of the
secular celebrations of shopping, gift wrapping, exchanging happy

smiles, and holiday feasts hold no appeal to me right now. I am dreading each day as it approaches, knowing each little thing will painfully remind me of my loss.

Marie had a love/hate relationship with Christmas, largely due to her depression. She would shop early, decorate, bake delicious cookies and complain every step of the way. Often, she would say, "Let's skip Christmas this year."
 Marie, this year I agree with you. Let's skip Christmas.

December 4, 2014
I don't want to live all alone
This house has too much room
There are sins for which I can't atone
All around is death and gloom
Our children are grown
They are no longer here
Far and wide they have flown
There is no holiday cheer
I am left here on my own
I need a lady by my side
To share an ice cream cone
And perhaps be my bride
The future is unknown
Someone may one day wear my ring
These lonely nights have clearly shown
Whatever the days ahead bring
I don't want to live alone.

December 5, 2014
I am filled with anger.

I am angry that the doctors could not help Marie. I am angry about the way the physician's assistant informed us of her diagnosis. I am angry about the way a second physician's assistant informed us the treatments were not effective and death was imminent. I am angry that the doctors waited so long to begin treatment. I am angry that they did not try another course of treatment. I am angry that other people get cancer and find a cure.

I am angry that I can't find a teaching job. I am angry that I am left to figure it out on my own. I am angry that Marie would not go to a doctor earlier. I am angry with God that He let this happen. I am angry that it is cold and won't stop snowing. I am angry that cancer exists.

I realize that everything happens for a reason. I do not blame the doctors for Marie's death; they did what they could. I don't blame school districts for not hiring me; there are younger candidates with more energy. I do not blame God for her death; I have faith He has a plan for me.

I still hate cancer. It has taken so many close to me. I will hate it and fight it as long as I breathe.

December 6, 2014
[I linked to the Hank Williams Sr. song, "I'm So Lonesome I Could Cry"]
Sometimes you just need to listen to a really sad song.

Music was always playing in our house and we shared similar musical tastes. We enjoyed going to concerts together. Some memorable shows we saw include the Doobie Brothers, James Taylor, Willie Nelson, and John Denver.

As we got older, and our family grew, Marie lost her taste for crowds. More and more, she allowed her depression to confine her to safe spaces. I refused to live in a self-imposed cage and continued to go to concerts. I would go with friends, my brother, and later, with my kids. I enjoyed introducing my kids to Willie Nelson, the Grateful Dead, and the Nitty Gritty Dirt Band. Cancer took Marie away from us. In a way, so did depression.

December 7, 2014
When you lose someone close to you, your world stops. Daily routines are discontinued. You walk the dog, because you have to. You bathe, dress, and eat because you have to. You meet with the mortician and make decisions because you have to.

The world becomes gray and sounds are muted. If the TV is on, it makes no sense, as if they are speaking a different language. Friends and relatives stop by to offer "anything they can do." Even in a crowded room, you feel alone.
It is almost as if you are in a sensory deprivation room. The only thing you feel is pain. What is really difficult to realize is that life goes on around you. Those not affected are working, playing, shopping, going about the business of life.

It is like stepping off a bus, standing on the curb, and watching the world go by. You walk as if you are in quicksand, each step a struggle.

Another concept difficult to grasp is that other people are also dealing with pain and loss. Someone lost a pet, someone else just had surgery, and yet another was diagnosed with cancer.

You expect everyone to know about your loss and to offer sympathy. I think when I realized other people were suffering and needed me to comfort them was when I started my return to the land of the living. I crawled out of the quicksand, cleaned myself up, and got back on the bus.

They say no man is an island, though sometimes you create one for yourself. Fortunately, I learned quickly that I was not meant to live on an island and my place was among the living. If you find yourself on Grief Island, find someone to help, to comfort. Open your broken heart to someone who is hurting. By helping them heal, you will begin to heal yourself.

You've seen the houses on the beach. They are built on stilts. If you live there, you can enjoy the ocean every day. The gentle lapping of the waves on the shore can lull you to sleep. Few things are more calming or peaceful. But every once in a while, a hurricane rolls in. The storm shakes the foundation, breaks windows, and moves piles of sand so the beach is no longer recognizable. What was once a safe relaxing haven is now a nightmare. Same house, same beach, same ocean and yet everything is different. Rebuild or walk away?

If you walk away, you have to start over somewhere else, taking only memories. If you stay, you are faced with lots of work and will be surrounded by memories. Will you ever feel safe there again? Will the memories of the devastation overwhelm you?

Losing a loved one is like that. You are lulled by the day to day routine of working and raising a family. You never dream that disease and death will upset your routine. When it does, your foundation is shaken, illusions of permanence shattered. You struggle to make sense of it all. At some point, you re-enter the land of the living. Same house, same friends, same neighborhood -- yet everything is different.

People who knew you as a couple struggle to deal with you alone. The house that you built no longer feels like home. It is a place of death. Painful memories of months of disease and death overshadow years of happy memories. Rebuild or walk away?

For me, there was no choice. Walk away, start over. Begin a new life, make new friends.

Your decision may be different. That's okay. Grief and our response to it is an individual thing. I guess my best advice would be to pray, listen for an answer, and trust your heart.

December 8, 2014
Does grief have a half life? You know, like radioactive material. Will I stop hurting in a month, a year, two years? Does it ever stop hurting? Will I one day wake up, go through my day, and not think of her? Will I be able to hear "Sweet Caroline" and not crumple up in pain?

I dread the coming holidays. I know everything will remind me of Marie. Everything will remind me that I am alone. Don't get me wrong -- I do not want to forget Marie. That would be impossible, as she will always be a part of who I am.

I do want to live again, breathe again, and smile again. I sincerely believe I would be dishonoring her memory by sitting in a corner alone and crying. She wanted me to go on without her. She knew her time was done and mine was not.

I don't know how much time I have; no one does. I don't know where I will be this time next year or where I will be working. I don't know if I will still be alone or once again have someone by my side. The only thing I do know is that it is in God's hands. I trust Him to take me where He needs me.

December 9, 2014
I think I am still in shock. I mean, a diagnosis on August 4 and death November 18? I barely had time to wrap my head around the fact that my wife had cancer. Now she's gone.
I am barely functioning. I eat because it's time to eat, not because I'm hungry. I run the vacuum because if I don't, no one else will. I feed and walk the dog. She seems just as confused as I am.

I am going through the motions, not really feeling anything. I know I will have to work again, but have no idea if I will be able to face a classroom of students. I go to church or have dinner with friends and still feel alone and lonely.

I think my finances are okay but don't really care. I can live in my motor home if I have to. How long will I plod along? How long before I feel anything but pain? How long before the clouds part and I once again see the Sun? God, I miss her.

<u>December 10, 2014</u>
When I tell people what happened to my wife, many say "I have no words." or, "I don't know what to say."

It's okay. I don't know what to say either, or for that matter, what I want to hear.

Suggestions: 1) "She is with God." 2) "Let me give you a hug."

My faith is very important to me. I have a theory about God in our lives and had the opportunity give witness to it in a church service. I believe that we are all born with an empty cup. We are also born with a yearning to fill that cup. Some people try to fill it with money or possessions. Some try drugs or alcohol. Others try to fill it with dangerous activities. All of these attempts to fill the cup come up short and leave a longing, a sense of something missing.

There is one thing that will fill the cup and satisfy the soul: the love of and for God. When you give yourself over to God and put your trust in Him, you begin to feel His love. The more you experience this, the more you love Him. As this love grows, the cup fills and the soul is satisfied. What's in your cup?

<u>December 11, 2014</u>
Solitary Man
We were together
For so many years
We were able to weather
A great many tears
Troubles are easy to face
When you are two
You do it with grace
Walking, as if in one shoe
We climbed the hills
And swam in the valleys
Roller coaster thrills
And bowling alleys
We were a team
Together forever
Or so it would seem
Now it's but a dream
And I'm all alone
Walking the beam
My heart a cold stone

How could this be
This wasn't the plan
Now it's just me
A solitary man

December 12, 2014
Ours was not a perfect marriage. Whose is? We had are struggles.
Who doesn't?

Many of our problems came down to communication, or lack of
it.

"Why are you angry?"
"If you don't know, I'm certainly not going to tell you."

What does that accomplish? If something is bothering you, say
something. When it comes right down to it, men and women are
different. (Vive la difference!) We think differently and we
communicate differently. Men are problem-solvers. If someone
comes to me with a situation, I think about it and suggest a
solution. Tell me someone is giving you a hard time, I'll offer to
bash their head in. It's hard to get past that caveman thing.

Women, so I'm told, do not want that! When they have a
problem, they want to talk about it. They want someone to listen
and say things like, "That is awful" or, "I can understand why that
would upset you."

Even being in possession of this valuable knowledge, I still have
to fight to suppress the urge to solve problems for women.

Our marriage had its ups and downs. Through it all though, we were a
team. When something good happened to one of us, we both celebrated.
If one of us got knocked down, the other was there with support and
encouragement.

Marie would receive a promotion or raise, and we would celebrate. I
would lose a job, and she would tell me not to worry, that something
better would come along. It always did.

Over the course of a few years, Marie's car was hit by a person
without insurance, a drunk driver, and several deer -- never her fault. Her
response was always, "I can't have anything nice." She would always end
up with a new car or one repaired good as new. My job was to try to keep

her calm through the process. Divorce was never an option for either of us.

I truly believe that both of us felt that God meant for us to be together. We took that whole "til death do us part" thing seriously. Weddings are joyous times. Marriage is tough. Both of you have to work at it, together. We did, and I am glad.

December 13, 2014
Nighttime is definitely the hardest. During the day, I do chores, shop, walk the dog, visit, anything to keep myself moving and not thinking. At night, I am forced to face reality. I can turn on the TV or blast the stereo, but I'm still alone. I talk to Lady; she's hurting too.

We built this house together and everything in it reminds me of her and that she is gone. I am not looking for pity. I'm not the only one who ever lost a spouse. I just want someone to talk to. I just want someone to tell me I will be okay. I just want someone to hold me while I cry.

December 14, 2014
Normally, the house would be decorated for Christmas, inside and out. There would have been a tree and colored lights brightening even the darkest corners. The house would smell of fresh baked cookies. There would be shopping and wrapping. There would be scheduling all our visits to family and friends. None of that is happening this year. All the other houses in the neighborhood are brightly lit while our house is dark.

Our house. It is still OUR house. Our house is dark, like my mood. I don't feel merry. I don't feel like visiting friends. I don't feel like giving or getting presents. Just fly over this year, Santa.

December 15, 2014
Marie's urn is in a place of honor. It is on a table with her picture and a wreath. She is gone, but she is still here. I can't fathom how what was once the girl I loved now sits in a tiny jar.

She will travel to Canada with Brad and I in a few days. She will stay with Kristy and Lucas until we can make arrangements to fulfill her wish of being buried at sea.

December 16, 2014
I am tied by the chains of grief
I can't smile or go for a walk
My life stolen by a thief
I can't sing or even talk
I'm a prisoner in my own house
You ask me why
I just lost my spouse
Now I just cry
I struggle against the chain
Why can't people see
That I am in such pain
And just want to be free
I did not die
and yet I am dead
I want to know why
I can't use my head
My thoughts are clouded
My heart is frozen
My emotions are shrouded
In this cloak I have chosen
I want to break out
To once again feel
I need to shout
This cannot be real

December 17, 2014
Next week we'll be heading for Canada. I have to buy and wrap
presents. I have to get the car ready for the trip. I have to get
passports, food, water, etc. for the trip. I have to... I have to…

December 18, 2014
This is the first time in 32 years there is no tree for Christmas.
The first time there are no light displays outside. The first time in
40 years Marie is not with me to celebrate.

I am looking forward to being with Brad, Kristy, and Lucas. I am
not feeling like celebrating.

December 19, 2014
I sit alone in the dark
Too late for a walk in the park
I should be sleepy

But I am too weepy
The empty house groaning
Or was it me moaning
The floor creaks
Nobody speaks
I stare at the empty bed
The spot where she laid her head
I complained about her snore
Now I will hear it no more
It's funny the things I will miss
As I remember our last kiss
The smell of her hair
How we made a great pair
The aromas in the kitchen
How she would take time to listen
She would fight through her fear
And say just hold me near
She would comfort those who lost
Without a care to the cost
She would try to talk through her laughter
And we would smile about it after
It was rare, I think
That she ever took a drink
And thought it a joke
If someone asked her to smoke
She loved her pet
Lady was the best yet
Anyone could see
That she truly loved me
And as hard as I try
I can't figure out why
She made me a better man
Now I'm doing the best that I can
Alone in the dark gloom
Of this now empty room.

December 20, 2014
I move through the quiet, dark house
In the dead of night
tears keep me awake
The sting of death's bite
Is the only feeling
She is gone a few days
And I am left reeling

How can this be
that I am alone
my life shattered on the rocks
my heart a cold stone
I want to wake from my dreams
To find it is not
All that it seems
That she is still here
I want to awake
and find her near
Though I cannot wake up
If I never sleep
The nightmare will never break up
I walk in the night
By myself, all alone
Filled with the fright
That tomorrow will be the same

December 21, 2014
Going through life day by day
Taking whatever comes my way
Some good some bad
Some happy some sad
Never knowing tomorrow
Will be filled with sorrow
We complain
About some minor pain
Or about the notion
I didn't get the promotion
Or start crying woe
Because I stubbed my toe
We don't realize
That today's sunny skies
Will be replaced with rain
Our hearts seared with pain
We should make a vow
Let's start right now
To celebrate little things
To look for joy that life brings
To follow after
Whatever brings laughter
To never put anything above
Those you truly love

December 22, 2014

We are heading north to spend Christmas with my daughter and son-in-law. Brad and I are driving there over the next two days. Neither of us want to be in our home. It just feels empty without Marie.

December 23, 2014

Christmas is a joyful time, a time to celebrate God's love for us. It is a celebration of His gift of eternal life to us, in the form of His son.

This year, it does not feel joyful. It does not feel like a celebration.

Though normally I feel God's presence and love in my life, right now, I am in a cold, dark place, feeling very unloved. I feel empty, alone, and without direction. This is a place that is very foreign to me as I am usually happy and optimistic. I don't know how long this will last. I do know that I do not want to become comfortable here. I do not want to live in a cold, gray world.

Marie is gone. I can't change that. I know it is my choice how I spend my days. Should I curl up, cry in the corner, and be an object of pity? Or should I stand up, count my blessings, and use my gifts to help others? Again, I don't know how long I will be here. I do know I am only visiting.

December 24, 2014

Merry Christmas to all from the Great White North. (I'm visiting my daughter and son-in-law in Canada.)

Christmas! Christmas was by far her favorite time of the year. Though she would grumble and say things like, "Let's skip Christmas." she loved it. Preparations included shopping for presents that seemed to begin on Boxing Day. She would buy presents and squirrel them away in her secret hiding places. Sometimes, she would buy an item twice, forgetting a previous purchase.

Next up was the cookies. Marie and her sister started baking and freezing cookies in September or early October. They made dozens of dozens of varieties, all of them delicious. Most were given as gifts to friends, relatives, and coworkers. This was just another example of Marie putting others before herself. She would spend hours prepping, baking, and arranging cookies on plates which would be emptied in minutes. I really miss her cookies.

Final preparations for the big day involved decorating the home. She would direct me in the installation of the exterior light display while she transformed the interior into a winter wonderland. Her perfectionist spirit was never as evident as when she was decorating. She would tie and retie a ribbon for over an hour until it was just so.

It was my responsibility to erect the tree and then get out of the way. If I strung the lights on the tree, she would redo them to her satisfaction. Time after time, I would tell her, "Perfect is the enemy of good." It was to no avail. Decorations had to be symmetrical, light cords could not be in evidence, and two Christmas balls of the same color could not hang next to each other.

Every year, friends and relatives would say, "That is the prettiest Christmas tree ever!" And that was why she loved Christmas. Seeing other people enjoy her decorations, watching people open their gifts from her, or hearing the oohs and ahhs of people eating her cookies. It was always about other people's joy over her own.

December 25, 2014
The first Christmas present did not come wrapped in paper and bows
Jesus came wrapped in swaddling clothes
He never wore a ring
He never owned anything
He came to show us the way
Our debt for sin to pay
Now we spend our time in malls
Looking for things to deck the halls
We shop and shop for piles of stuff
When will someone say,"Enough!"?
Let's go back to the lesson He taught us
And not hope for things people bought us
Let's love one another
And be kind to our brother
Instead of buying toys
Let's be good girls and boys
Do a good deed

Help someone in need
Your treasure is like a used tissue
When all's said and done, you can't take it with you
Give up the fight
Forgive those who spite
Apologize to those you hurt
Let Heaven know you're on alert
Keep your eyes
On the prize
For the day will come
And He will take you Home

Merry Christmas!

Brad and I found a church with a Christmas Eve service last night.
The people were warm and welcoming. The pastor was from
Pennsylvania. While I am still not in the Christmas spirit, I'm glad
we went. All things considered, we still have much for which to be
thankful. After church, we enjoyed a feast of fresh lobsters. Today
we opened presents and shared memories of Marie.

December 26, 2014
Happy Boxing Day! Whatever that is.
I don't know why Marie had to die
I don't know why I was left to cry
I look to the sky for an answer
Why did Marie get cancer
I don't know why I'm all alone
I don't know why my heart is like a stone
I pray to God for rest
Why am I put to the test
I don't know why my kids lost their Mom
I don't know when peace will come
I ask my friends for a hug
Why do some only shrug
I don't know if I will ever teach
I don't know if it's true what they preach
I go to my church seeking healing
Why does my heart have no feeling
I don't know what the future will bring
I don't know if someone new will wear my ring
I search my soul
When will I crawl out of this hole?

A cold, white blanket covers the Earth. Nothing moves, as if time itself is frozen. Marie is only a memory, a hint of perfume.

Pictures tell a story of happier times. Memories bring laughter or tears. Soon, Brad and I will head back to Pennsylvania. He will return to State College. Lady and I will be left to begin again.

I am woefully unprepared to deal with everything. Marie and I worked as a team. Now I am on my own trying to figure it out. There is no training manual. They don't teach this in school. There are grief counseling sessions available, but I don't want to be around other sad people.

Like everyone else, I need a raison d'etre, a reason to be. I want to be of value to someone. I am not one to worry. On the other hand, Marie was the major breadwinner. I won't be able to support my lifestyle as a substitute teacher.

That's the simple reality of the situation. If I can't find a job teaching full-time, I will have to look for another career or look for a teaching job in another state. Part of me understands this cold, hard truth. Another part of me says I am in no condition to be making life-changing decisions.

A few months ago, I said there will be time for tears in the future. Well, the future is here. For now, I will cry.

December 28, 2014
Did you ever wish you could go back to a certain point in your life and change a decision you made?

As a senior in high school, I had to choose between a part-time job and football. I chose the job, as the money meant a taste of independence. Stupid move. Our team went undefeated and won the State championship. Although I later coached, I never played football again.

Marie and I met at a skating rink. After skating together for a short while, I told her we would marry someday. Smart move.

We would take family vacations. She would go to the beach, I would play golf. Stupid move.

After working at my first job for two years, I quit so we could move back to be closer to our families. Smart move.

I guess the point is that hindsight is 20/20. If I could go back and change things, I would have spent more time with Marie.

December 29, 2014
Gray clouds dust the skies
And threaten rain
Tears fall from my eyes
I can't hide the pain
When you lose your wife
Who was oh so young
It changes your life
Your heart has been stung
You want to stop and go back
To who knows when
We could live in a shack
If we could just do it again
We'll get right this time
I'll make a solemn vow
If we're down to our last dime
I'll treat you right somehow
Together we will stand
We'll show the whole world
I'll hold your hand
And love my beautiful girl
Before things unravel
And my heart turns blue
The world we'll travel
Just me and you
We'll see every sight
We long to see
We'll dance in the night
Just you and me
Instead, reality I face
I see an empty pillow
She's gone without a trace
Like the leaves of a willow
In the dead of winter
I'll make a new start
Though my memories splinter
She's forever in my heart

Time
We'll do it next year
I promise you, honey
Don't worry dear
We'll save enough money
I can't leave my job
The kids are too small
And the beach is a mob
Next year we'll do it all
We can't afford a vacation
The car needs new brakes
Next year, we'll travel the nation
For Heaven's sakes
Why such a hurry
We'll all still be here
No need to worry
We can do it next year
We'll get in the car and go
To the state of Nebraska
Brag to everyone you know
And we'll go to Alaska
Or, maybe not
Hold on a sec
You know that plan you got
There's something you didn't check
You know the answer?
You saved every dime
Now your wife has cancer
And you're all out of time.

In school, I watch for teachable moments. Kids especially do not understand the value of time. I explain that if they lose a toy, they can get a new one. If someone steals their money, they can work and get more. If however, they waste time in class, that time is gone and can't be replaced.

Time is our most precious commodity. Unfortunately, that is wisdom that usually comes too late.

December 31, 1972, I met a young lady. That night, I told her that I would one day ask her to marry me. We spent 42 years together, 36 as man and wife. Cancer took her away from me in November.

I am ready to be done with 2014. I am confident that God has a better year planned for me in 2015. Happy New Year to all.

January 1, 2015
And thus begins not only a new chapter in my life story but a whole new book. I believe it will be an adventure with a happy ending. Happy New Year, everyone.

We moved several times when I was young. As we moved, I noticed and picked up the various regional accents and colloquialisms. I found that the quicker you sounded like your neighbors, the more quickly you were accepted.

I also watched Jonathan Winters and Robin Williams on TV. I loved how they used their voices to become different characters. When Kristy was young, I often spoke using different European accents. I stopped when one of her friends asked her, "What country is your dad from?"

I also enjoyed spinning tall tales and seeing if I could get the kids to buy into them. On a trip to Myrtle Beach, I explained that it used to be a bay. It was then used as a garbage dump. They piled garbage and soil in layers until the bay was filled in. Then they trucked in sand from various beaches. And now, it is the beautiful vacation spot we all love. They completely bought it.

When I told them that Nazis used human tattoos to make lampshades (which they did) they said I was making it up. For some reason, they always believed my stories, but did not believe facts.

January 2, 2015
Two young people meet and join together
They walk hand in hand through all kinds of weather
They share the joys that life brings
They hold each other during scary things
They work every day to pay the bills
And nurse the other through their ills
One by one the days go by
Years go by in the blink of an eye
A daughter comes to brighten our days
We both love her in so many ways
And then came a boy
Who doubled our joy

The kids skinned their knees
And brought home dogs with fleas
The kids both grew
And away from home they flew
Now it's just Marie and me
We've got the whole world to see
On a cruise to Bermuda
We'll catch barracuda
We'll see faraway places
With smiles on our faces
Nothing will stand in our way
Until we hear the doctor say
"You have cancer."

January 3, 2015
I just had a very pleasant online chat with a very nice lady. I have a
good feeling about 2015.

I know, I know. I am being cautious. There is no meeting set up
and I'm not sending her a check! And for those of you who think
it's too soon, I'm 58. How long do you want me to wait?

Thanks for listening. I feel better now. And we're three days into
the new year and I haven't posted a political rant. How do you like
the new me?

I have spent very little time alone in my life. I don't like being alone.
I'm just not wired that way. I knew that I did not want to try to pick up
girls at the bar -- that's not where you meet the kind of girl I was looking
for. All the attractive women at my church were already spoken for. I was
lonely. I decided to try online.

I have mixed feelings about the process. On one hand, looking at
pictures of lovely women can be exciting, imagining the possibilities. On
the other hand, it is a little dehumanizing, almost like grocery shopping.
While I wanted an attractive lady, it was also important that she was
mature and stable. I didn't want someone who needed me; I wanted
someone who wanted me. I began my foray into modern dating.

The online chats were with two different girls on a dating website. I
had good conversations -- text only -- with both of them. Before I had
the chance to meet either, I revealed my situation, that I had very recently
been widowed. Both got spooked and said it was way too soon for me to
get involved. They never took the chance to get to know me. Marie knew I
was not meant to be alone and had told me to find someone new.

I got mixed responses from my friends. Some were thrilled that I was determined not to be alone. Others couldn't see me with anyone but Marie. My children were aghast that I could even consider having feelings for someone other than their mother.

<u>January 4, 2015</u>
I lost my wife of many years
Days of work and nights of tears.
I roam my empty house
As quiet as a mouse.
Living under a shroud
Gray sky covered in cloud.
I have dreams about my new life
I want to share them with my new wife.
I know one day I will again see the Sun
With a new Love, will you be the One?
(sometimes poetry is the only way to express your feelings)

When we were raising our kids, vacations usually meant a trip to beach. Several of those trips involved our brothers' and our friends' families. One of our favorite destinations was Myrtle Beach. Sometimes we would rent a large condo; sometimes we took a caravan of campers.

On most of these trips, the men would golf while the women and children went to the beach. We would all meet up for dinner and game nights after. During every trip, I would say that we should move down to Myrtle Beach and get out of the snow. Marie would have none of it. She would not leave Pennsylvania.

<u>January 5, 2015</u>
I have heard it said that death takes a person from us in bits and pieces. Yes, the person you loved is suddenly gone. However, you have physical reminders -- her clothes, her jewelry, pictures. You can catch her scent on her clothes. You have memories of her smile, the sound of her voice and her laughter.

In time, the clothes are donated and jewelry is given to friends and relatives. Memories fade over time. You lose the smell of her hair, the tinkle of her laughter. You still have the pictures, but wish you had video with her talking.

January 6, 2015
Since my love has gone
I am an empty shell
Together for so long
Now I walk alone in Hell
I chew my tasteless food
I cannot see the Sun
Even strangers know my mood
Left foot, right, left foot, right
I trudge along through the day
Into the lonely night
Will I ever find a way
To smile once more
Will my heart at last
Stop aching to its core
I write the check to pay my bill
And hope the money's there
It gives me no thrill
To say I don't really care
I am a lost, lonely man
Feeling deaf and dumb
Doing what I can
Only feeling numb
She has gone to meet her maker
Each night I sit and pray
That God will take her
And we'll meet again someday.

When you suffer a terrible loss and the pain is crushing you, your body and mind try to protect you by going numb. You find yourself going through the motions of life. You shop, you cook, and you eat. You just don't feel anything, you don't taste anything.

Food is food. It could be a peanut butter and jelly sandwich or filet and lobster; it just doesn't matter. It could be a beautiful sunny day and all you'll see is clouds. You listen to the radio -- rap, rock, gospel -- it all sounds the same: sad. You turn on the TV and mindlessly watch someone extolling the virtues of non-stick cookware. People try to talk with you but give up when they realize you can't hear. Time loses meaning. What time is it? What day is it? You really don't care.

I don't know if this is a universal phenomenon. I don't know how long this numbness lasts or how long I spent being numb. I do know that it passes, and life does go on.

January 7, 2015
I just want to be free
To live the life God planned for me
No one else walks in my shoes
No one else pays my dues
Before giving me advice
I'll ask you to think twice
Is your life all it seems
Are you living your dreams
Walk my walk
Before you talk
Before you start
Look in your heart
And if you really care
A smile and hug you'll share
I lost my wife
But I still have life
If you haven't lost
You don't know the cost
I've had to pay
To find a new way
I am hoping only
To not live my life lonely

January 8, 2015
Sunshine is returning to my life. I enjoyed having dinner last night
with a high school classmate. It has been quite a while since I
laughed so much. Today I was assigned to a third grade classroom.
In the middle of class, while they were working on an art project,
a little girl raised her hand. When I called on her, she said, "I love
you Mr. M." I love teaching!

I returned to work, substitute teaching, right after Christmas break.
The summer before, I'd had a high school reunion -- an outdoor picnic
with food, music, and stories of the good old days. I reconnected with
people I hadn't seen in 40 years. A few of us decided to have a follow-up
mini-reunion in January at a local honky-tonk. A girl I hadn't seen since
high school was there.

In fifth grade, I had been the shortest kid in the class. Add dorky
glasses and a crew cut. I might as well have had a sign painted on my
forehead saying, "Bully me, please!" There seemed to be a line of kids
waiting to call me names or beat me up.

The tallest person in our class happened to be a cute girl. She was cute, but also one of the bullies in line to pick on me and she was a foot taller than me. One day, on the playground, it was her turn.

She started in on me and I decided it was time to make a stand. I took a mighty swing. I thought I had missed until I saw blood coming from her nose. I knew that I was in big trouble. Not only had I hit a classmate, I hit a girl! I had to spend some time after school with the teacher. After my time was up, he said, "You can go now."

Go? I was nine years old and ten miles from home. Both of my parents worked. I made several phone calls (using the office phone, since cell phones did not exist) to neighbors until I finally found someone willing to pick me up. I learned my lesson and I haven't hit a girl since. I wonder what would happen if a teacher did something like that today.

The tall girl and I had sat next to each other in homerooms all the way through high school, not liking each other. Her name was Cynthia. And here she was again.

We were both in jeans. She was visiting from Florida and not used to the cold Pennsylvania winter. She was vivacious -- the life of the party. That same feeling I had when I first saw Marie hit me again. I had to get to know this girl.

I asked her to dinner later in the week at Prime steakhouse. I got there before her and placed a rose on the table, just being a gentleman. She came in, saw the rose and said, "Is this a date?"

She then proceeded to tell me stories about her family and we ate and laughed and forgot our problems for a time. Her mother had passed away about the same time Marie did. I didn't know it at the time, but she was also going through a divorce. I walked her to her car in the bitter cold. I was hoping for at least a hug, as I thought the evening went very well. She opened the door, jumped in, closed it, and waved bye.

I called her the next day and asked if I had done something wrong. She said no, she was just trying to get out of the cold. I knew before she did that we would be together soon.

Our church in Nazareth did small-group book studies over the years. The message from one such study was this; you can't walk on water if you don't step out of the boat. Great things will not happen without the faith to take a risk. That message has stuck with me and guided my decision making since then.

If there is something you want to do, something that is calling you, have a little faith. Step out of the boat. Make it happen.

January 9, 2015
Today's poem:
Marie and the Night
The World is asleep, but not me,
No, not me.
My cheeks are burning with salty tears,
I lost the woman I loved all my years.
My dog and I are finding new ways
Of filling the hours of lonely days.
Nights, though, I find are the hardest of all
There's no one beside me, no one at all.
In the dark and all alone.
No one to talk to, no one to phone.
Tired, so tired yet sleep will not come.
I'm in pain, and yet I feel numb.
Still, I will not quit, I have much to give.
In the morning, the Sun will come up and I will live.

In my quest to become a teacher, I think that God has been trying
teach me patience. He has been trying for about four years now. I
wish He would hurry up.

January 10, 2015
Today's thoughts:
Chapter 2
And thus begins chapter two
A time for letting go
Exploring new possibilities
Letting go
Not forgetting
Beginning again
With more wisdom
With more passion
Where will life lead me
Who will walk beside me
No one is promised tomorrow
Today is the day
Life is precious
Laughter is music
Love is a treasure
Today Live
Today Laugh
Today Love!

January 11, 2015
The Christmas Tree
You go through life, day after day, working and paying the bills. You deal with the everyday ups and downs. Then Christmas season arrives.

You go out into the woods and search and search for the "perfect" tree. You find it and take it home. You put it in a special place in your home. Then decorations are added: balls, bells, and snowflakes. An angel or star becomes its hat. For weeks, you admire its beauty and luxuriate in its wonderful smell. You want it to stay forever. It is the best tree ever and you cherish it.

In time, though, you notice the needles changing color, some begin to fall. Sugar water is given to no avail. At some point you have to accept that it is time for the tree to come down. The decorations are removed and carefully stored for next season. The tree is bagged and removed from your home. Needles are swept up and furniture is moved. Weeks later, it's as if it was never there.

One day, you happen to step on a needle that was missed on cleaning day. It is a small painful reminder of the beauty that was once in your home. The memory of the loss brings a tear. Another day, a hint of pine scent comes out of nowhere and you smile at the conjured memory.

Life goes on and you go through life, day after day. You wait for next Christmas, and, though you will never forget your first tree, a brand new tree to cherish.

Every time I posted a poem, someone would comment, "You should write a book." I had committed to chronicling my healing for a year, and doing just that.

January 12, 2015
After committing to a year-long project of writing musings/poems about my healing process, I began to feel a little pressure. I started to understand how writers experience writer's block.

I did two things. First, I reminded myself to stick to the subject, me, my healing. No politics and no random ramblings. Second, and most importantly, I prayed that God would daily provide inspiration as He did yesterday.

Minutes later, I happened to look out my front window. I saw a lone bird stop at the bird feeder which has been empty for six months. Filling it is one of the things that I neglected in this process. I realized that no matter where you are on your journey, you are always in a position to help someone or something less fortunate than yourself. Excuse me, I have to go fill the feeder.

Thank you, God and thank you friends. Live. Laugh. Love.

January 13, 2015
Unanswered Questions, Unspoken Prayers
I'm living a life of unanswered questions
Why did she die?
Did I do everything I could?
Will I find a teaching job?
Where will I be living this time next year?
Will I find a new love?
Some answers will come in time, others will remain unanswered.
I ask God for answers.
I know what I want, He knows what I need.
I asked for a job, He said, "No, I need you to care for Marie."
I asked for Marie to beat cancer, He said, "No, I need her in Heaven."
Although, at times, it seems cruel and wrong, I've learned to trust Him.
He always puts me where I need to be.
He gives me the tools I need.
I have learned to trust Him to put me where He needs me to be.
I am in Your hands, Lord. Please answer my unspoken prayers.

I have already made clear my thoughts about worry: I have no time for it. Whenever I look at my bank statement and wonder if there is enough to cover retirement, I repeat: "Never worry about money. Whenever you get extra money, God will give you a bill to take care of it."

Throughout my life, I've received unexpected gifts, bonuses from work, and larger-than-expected tax returns. Shortly after each of these windfalls, an unexpected bill followed. The car needed new tires, college tuition for one of the kids, broken glasses, etc. Some people made comments like, "That sucks that you weren't able to enjoy the money." I was always grateful that our needs had been met.

Unspoken Prayers, Part 2
After a crushing life event, you have two choices: curl up in a ball
and cry, or, live your life. I choose to live my life. I find it helps to
count my blessings.
Thank you God for sons and daughters,
and for eagles and otters.
Thank you for green grass and blue skies,
and for strawberries and apple pies.
Thank you for moonlight and romance,
And for women who love to dance.
I never prayed for any of these things. They are all answers to
unspoken prayers.
Live. Laugh. Love.

I just read a story about a guy rescuing a snake from a fire, only to get
bitten. He does it again and again until a friend asks him why he continues
to help the snake when the snake bites him every time. He responded that
the way the snake treats him has no effect on the kind of person he is.
People have asked me why I am so nice to people even when they treat me
badly. I refuse to allow someone to change who I am. I was taught to treat
others with respect, to treat them the way I want to be treated. This means
I am sometimes taken advantage of or mistreated.

For example, I was taught to open the door for ladies. Many times, I
will hold it, and a lady will walk through but not acknowledge me. I could
get nasty and say, "At least say thank you!" Other times, I've been yelled at:
"I'm not helpless, I can open my own door!" I continue to hold doors
open. They will not change me.

Many years ago, a teacher took another student's word that I had done
something wrong in his absence. He never asked my side. He picked me
up off the floor by my ear, causing long-term hearing loss. I simply took it
and went on with my life. (He later died of cancer.)

In the end, I will be at peace knowing that I stayed true to myself.

January 15, 2015
Lucky
That was our word. Every birthday, anniversary, or Valentine's
Day card had to have the word "lucky" in it. It was a running joke
between us.
"I'm the lucky one."
"No, I'm the lucky one."

In reality, as in any long-term relationship, we began to see and focus on each others' faults. She snores and keeps me awake; she is bossy; she doesn't do fun things with me, etc.

At Marie's memorial service, I sat and listened as, one by one the speakers talked of what a remarkable woman she was. She always put others' happiness before her own. She made great cookies. She was intelligent. She always showed great empathy and was easy to talk to.

I realized then that I truly had been lucky to have her by my side all those years. As Joni Mitchell said, "You don't know what you've got 'til it's gone." I know now the next time I fall in love, I will close my eyes to her faults and shine a spotlight on what makes her special. I won't make the same mistake twice.

About the same time as my dissatisfaction with my job grew, we discovered that Marie was pregnant with our first child. With little money in the bank and no job prospects, I quit my job and we moved to an apartment in Allentown to be close to our families.

Shortly after our daughter, Kristy, was born we decided to look for a home. As I mentioned, her grandparents' farm had been parceled into building lots for aunts and uncles. There was one two-acre lot which still belonged to her parents. They sold it to us for one dollar.

It was there we built our house, in sight of the home where Marie had grown up. Over the years, I added two bedrooms and a bath to the upstairs. I built a covered porch on the front of the house. We added an addition with a two-car garage. The last addition was a beautiful deck that I built on the back of the house. On nice days, we would eat dinner on the deck while watching the deer in the field behind our house.

She died in that house. As much as that house was the result of my money, sweat, and blood, and as many good memories that house held, the freshest memories were of her illness and death. It was no longer my home and it would soon be time for a change.

The Computer and Healing
The computer... Is it a blessing or a curse? It has become my constant companion since Marie's death. (Lady, my collie, is jealous.) I bounce between Facebook, my email account, Ourtime.com, and school district websites. I'm searching for friendship, a life partner, and a full-time teaching position.

I find there is a dichotomy. On one hand, I find solace and companionship in the supportive comments from friends, relatives, and prospective life partners. On the other hand, there is no other hand. What I mean is there is no hand to hold.

There are no hugs (other than an occasional emoticon hug), kisses, or shoulders to cry on. You can spend hours "chatting" online getting to know someone, without really getting to know them. As powerful as the printed word can be, it cannot convey the nuances of voice inflection and facial expression. I am looking forward to finding my new soulmate and my first teaching position so that I can disconnect from the cyber world and reconnect with real people.

Kristy followed in her mom's footsteps by twirling in high school and earned the respect of coaches and teammates by her hard work and dedication. I always hated sitting through hours of watching other kids perform just so I could see my daughter's three-minute routine. I had better things to do.

Looking back, I should have treasured those times and treated my daughter better. She followed me to Penn State and became president of the actuarial society. She graduated and works as a consultant. Kristy married a Temple grad, Lucas, and moved to Canada where they enjoy ice climbing and mountain biking.

Bradley followed in my footsteps by riding the bench on his high school football team. Marie called him "Peanut" and loved him dearly. Even so, they fought constantly. She was always worried about him not finding his way. I assured her again and again that he would be able to stand on his own two feet.

After struggling in college and jumping from job to job, he has settled in to a management position at a nice restaurant in State College. I am proud of him and I know Marie is too. Brad enjoys playing goalie for a local soccer club, and he and I get together for an occasional round of golf.

Wisdom from a Rat
Yesterday, in school, I happened upon three quotes. One is from the movie Ratatouille, and two are from a book of famous quotes. Gusteau, the chef (ghost) in Ratatouille, said, "If you focus on what is left behind, you will never see what lies ahead."

A quote attributed to Alexander Graham Bell is as follows, "Sometimes we stare so long at a door that is closing, that we see too late the one that is open."

An unknown quipster put it simply, "Never let yesterday use up today."

It seems that these are merely different ways of expressing the same idea. They fit very nicely into my philosophy and my healing process. We can choose to dwell on the hurt and pain of what is past or lost or we can focus on creating a better and brighter future.

I still love Marie. Every minute of every day I wish I could talk to her, see her smile, or simply hold her close. I cannot live there. There is only death and tears. I choose life, laughter, and the hope of new love. Live, laugh, and love -- today.

In this age of electronics, it is amazing and incredibly sad that I do not have one recording of Marie's voice. I have only memories on that score.

While she suffered from depression and frequent migraine headaches, there were still times of smiles and laughter. One of my favorite memories of her is that she could not tell a joke. She would be so amused by the punch line, she would begin giggling halfway through the joke. By the time she would get to the end, she was reduced to squeaky, giggling noises. I never heard the end of her jokes but they always made me smile.

Her joy was rare but infectious. Some of my favorite moments came when I had no idea what she was saying. To see her happy always made my day. Most of these moments came after a drink or two while camping. What I would give to have a video of her telling a joke and ending in squeaky giggles.

Greatest Husband in the World
Marie worked with me. She taught me how to dress stylishly, to eat without offending tablemates, how to be a responsible adult. Just like every woman, she found the "perfect" guy and then went about changing me.

Although she did accomplish much good in this endeavor, I was not the "Greatest Husband in the World." (Anyone want to lay claim to that title?) I am human. I have my faults. I made my mistakes.

I wanted to tell Marie how very sorry I was for not being her "white knight on a steed," for not being there for her when she needed me, for not being the "Greatest Husband in the World."

I said, "Marie, I'm sorry for not being the best husband I could be." Her slurred (due to the combination of the cancer and the medication) response was, "Shut up." It was her way of telling me that it was not the time for recriminations.

I said, "I love you."
She replied, "I love you, too."

We kissed. It was the last thing she said to me and it was our last kiss.
I have to stop, my keyboard is flooded.

January 19, 2015
Grief is Overrated
This grief thing, there's nothing to it. I'm cooking, cleaning, working, doing laundry, taking care of my dog, and losing weight. I'm getting all kinds of support (and hugs) from friends, new and old. The sun came out and happiness is returning. It's all good.

Yeah, right.

Yesterday, our church camping group had a potluck dinner to plan this season's outings. I made ham and string beans (I said I can cook, didn't I?). I put it in the crock pot, put the crock pot in the carrier, and headed to my car. I began to load it on to the back seat, as I always did before.

That's when I remembered that every time I did that, Marie told me to put it on the floor so it would not fall if we had to brake suddenly. I dutifully set it on the floor (I told you she civilized me).

"There, are you happy?" I said. And the tears began.

There was a quick trip to the living room where I grabbed her picture and clutched it to my chest as I sobbed uncontrollably. I cried all the way to church and then some.

People asked how I was doing. All I could do was shrug.

The woman who leads our group lost her husband last year. She simply hugged me and said, "I know." Thank you, Sue.

As good and strong as I feel most of the time, I realize that I am still fragile and prone to leaking eyes at the slightest provocation. If you see me, hug me. Thank you. (My eyes are leaking again.)

January 20, 2015
Karaoke
As I have said in previous posts, I am fine during the day. My nights are often long, lonely, and sleepless.

Before Marie's death, I would occasionally go out and sing karaoke with friends. She rarely joined me as she preferred to stay at home and rest from her busy week. Since her passing, I use my weekly trip to the karaoke club as an escape. I try to sing at least one song in each session for her.

One was "Honey" by Bobby Goldsboro. (Go ahead and try to sing that after losing your spouse.) Another choice was Willie Nelson's "Always on my Mind." My friends were in tears because they knew the lyrics hit so close to home. (And, no they weren't crying because I butchered the song. I can do Willie.)

Saturday night, I chose the song "For the Good Times" written by Kris Kristofferson as performed by Ray Price. It was the song that was playing when Marie and I first skated together 42 years ago. I realized the haunting irony of that being our first song as I sang the second verse:

I'll get along, you'll find another
And I'll be here if you should find you ever need me
Don't say a word about tomorrow or forever
There'll be time enough for sadness when you leave me.

The judges on American Idol tell contestants that they have to "feel" the lyrics. I understand now what they mean. Yes, Kris, there will be time enough for sadness.

January 21, 2015
Possessions
I love *Reader's Digest* for its inspiring stories and its various humor sections. I tear through it each month. This month, there is a section called "Dear America," containing letters from people who serve in our military.

One Air Force major wrote: "People who live in one place tend to accumulate a lot of stuff—not us. In the military, you move all the time, and because your family is often separated, it puts into perspective what's important. You learn to focus not on possessions but on experiences."

Grief will do the same thing. I walk through my large, lonely house, looking at closets and drawers crammed full of "stuff." While neither of us were hoarders, in 36 years in the same place, you accumulate a lot of stuff. Part of my healing process will involve de-cluttering, getting rid of stuff, letting go. I spent hours today emptying a closet of stuff that I will never use. It will be donated to a church that runs a flea market as a fundraiser. I find it is time to focus more on experiences and friends and less on "stuff." Does anyone need a crock pot?

January 22, 2015
Early in our marriage, music used to fill our home. Neil Young, Bruce Springsteen, and other rockers' LPs shook our walls, making conversation next to impossible. Soon, with kids and jobs requiring early a.m. alarms, the music ended. Except for rare occasions, there was little music played. On those rare occasions, I was informed that it was too loud. I can't remember if I cried the day the music died.

Music is once again being played in my home. It is easier now. I put on a Sirius radio channel on the TV and we're good to go. No records, no turntable, and no scratchy noises from overplayed albums. I've been listening to The Bridge, a station dedicated to mellow music from the 60's and 70's. (My kids hate it.) Listening to it the other day, I realized that many of the artists on the station are no longer with us. Harry Chapin, John Denver, Jim Croce, and Joe Cocker are among the dear departed still getting airplay.

I thought about how some songs can transport you back to happier times, can evoke pleasant memories even though the singer is long dead. There will come a time when I will hear a song, look at a picture, or smell cookies baking that I will be reminded of Marie and think only happy thoughts.

I am not there yet. Unexpected triggers lurk everywhere. Alarms go off in my head; Flush Eyes! Gasp for breath! Crumple to your knees! Friends who have experienced similar losses tell me it gets a little easier each day. In the meantime, I have my music and my memories.

My family and I are all Penn State fans. Many of us are Penn State grads. Back in 2011, a huge scandal erupted over a former coach abusing children. Penn State lost its president, athletic director, and chief of campus police to the scandal. Along with the children, another victim of the scandal was Penn State head coach Joe Paterno.

In the midst of a media frenzy, someone other than a retired assistant coach had to fall. Joe was tried and convicted by the media. Ask anyone who is not a Penn State fan and you would think Joe committed the crime. Anyone who knew Joe and his family knows that Joe would never put up with someone hurting children.

Anyway, there has been enough written about the scandal. There are two reasons I am including this painful episode. First, when all this was going on, I thought it was the most painful thing I would ever experience, the trashing of my beloved Penn State and my hero, Joe. Three years later, I found out I was mistaken.

The second reason is that shortly after he was fired, it was announced that Joe had cancer. He left us on January 22, 2012. My son, being a lifelong fan, was among the thousands who attended his viewing. Joe's son Jay was in the receiving line. When Brad approached Jay, he broke into tears. Jay took him in his arms and comforted him. Joe was an amazing individual. He and Sue Paterno raised some amazing kids. Rest in peace, Joe. Cancer sucks.

<u>January 23, 2015</u>
One day this week, I substituted in a 6th grade classroom. The school was short subs and I was asked to cover a kindergarten class during my free period. My answer is always, "Wherever you need me and whatever you need me to do."

The children gathered around for the opening exercises of days of the week, the ABC song, and counting the number of days in school. Just before we began, a little girl came up to me and said, "Faith."

I asked, "Is that your name?"
She said "No, no one is named Faith, just faith."
I gave her a quizzical look and she said, "Faith in the Lord."
She then gave me a sweet smile and took her place with the other children.

Faith, indeed. It is Faith in the Lord that gives me strength and courage to face each day as I struggle to begin again. Our church has a saying, "God is still speaking." At times He speaks to us as we read the Bible. Sometimes we hear Him when a stranger performs an act of kindness. And, sometimes His messenger is a lovely young child.

<u>January 24, 2015</u>
The other day, I talked about music and musicians who are no longer with us. I talked about how, even though they are gone, they still bring us joy. Yesterday, I called my sister-in-law and got the answering machine. The voice on the machine was her recently deceased husband. It was nice to be able to hear his voice.

It then occurred to me that I do not have any recordings of Marie's voice. Yes, I have pictures and memories but I will never again hear her voice. How nice would it be when I am hurting to push a button and hear her speaking. In this age of technology, it's almost a crime to have let the opportunity to record a message from her slip away. (It is hard to see the keyboard through my tears.) Over the next few weeks, I will be taking a few selfie videos for my two children.

<u>January 25, 2015</u>
Up and Down
Glistening snowflakes
Oh, how my heart aches
Painful sorrow
With hope for tomorrow
Helpful friends
Sad that life ends
Missing my wife
Beginning a new life
Feel like I'm flying
Can't keep from crying
My life in tatters
Discovering what matters
Talk on the phone
Feeling alone
My moods up and down
Trying not to frown
Teary eyes
Starry skies
Help from Above
Live, Laugh, Love

<u>January 26, 2015</u>
Yesterday in church, I met with a friend (our retired pastor) who complimented me on my writing. I thanked him and explained that it was cathartic for me and was a very important part of my healing process. He observed that, judging from the many comments on my posts, it was helping others as well.

When you are grieving a terrible loss, it sometimes feels like you alone are dealing with sadness. I have to remind myself to be mindful of other people's feelings and to not selfishly expect everyone to care more about my hurt than their own. Everyone has lost someone close to them and has to find a way to deal with the pain.

If my writing, in some small way, helps others, it would help to give meaning to Marie's death. Anyone who knew Marie knows that she was all about helping others before herself. I can think of no better way to honor her memory than to give of myself to help someone else who is also hurting. Thank you, Dave.

January 27, 2015
Winter
Bitter cold. Fields blanketed in snow. Tree limbs, bare of leaves, rimmed in ice. Desolate, lifeless. But wait, beautiful birds are at the bird feeder and fresh tracks appear in the snow. Days are getting longer and, though more snow is in the forecast, there is hope for spring.

As the snow melts, it will seep into the ground or run off to replenish creeks and rivers. Animals will waken from their winter naps and return to the landscape. A sure sign of spring and new life will be the robin returning from her Southern vacation and once again occupying the nest on my front porch. Trees will bud, flowers will bloom, (my allergies will kick in) and life will return.

January 28, 2015
If/Maybe
If I knew then what I know now.
If I played more than one year of football.
If I had been a better student in college.
If I took more of an interest in my children's activities.
If I spent less time watching TV and more time talking to my wife.
If she went to the doctor about her back pain.
If we had gone to a different hospital for treatment.
If they started treatment earlier.
If, if, if…every life is full of "ifs".
If any one of those things changed, I would not be who I am today.
If any one of those things changed, I would not be where I am today.
If I trust God, new doors will be opened.
If I trust God, new blessings await.
Maybe this time, I'll get it right.

January 29, 2015
Longevity
About two years ago, Marie and I started arguing about who was going to go first. To me, the answer was always obvious: I would be the first.

Look at any actuarial table and you would realize that it had to be so. Females always outlive males. She never smoked and rarely drank. Most women in her family lived to 85 and beyond.

My father barely made 70 and his brothers died in their 60s. The idea that she would predecease me was ludicrous.

She had her mind made up. She claimed the stress from her job was much more taxing than anything her female relatives had experienced. I countered that she did not experience the Great Depression or the stresses of a World War. At the first diagnosis in August, she told me she would not see Christmas.
Again, I said that with prayer and treatments, she would see many more Christmases. One of her chief complaints about me was that I never listened to her. I guess she was right. I should have listened to her. It seems she had some inside information.

I decided to take a course and earn a Reading Specialist certificate as a way to make myself more marketable. Driving home from college tonight, I thought, "Hey, I have not cried today." So much for that.

January 30, 2015
Robin
I mentioned in an earlier post that my writing has played a huge part in my healing process. I believe that, when grieving, you will pay the price. What I mean is that you will have your down times, your quiet moments of anguish. Some people try to avoid them by staying busy all the time. They are simply delaying payment.

From day one, I have allowed myself time to be alone, time with my memories, time with pictures of Marie, and times to cry. Writing on a daily basis has forced me to really think about the grief process, to face it, to live it, and not try to avoid it. I am not done grieving but I am making progress.

Another huge part of my healing process is a high school classmate. Our class reunion took place last summer, shortly after Marie's initial diagnosis. The event stirred many of us to reconnect, mostly through Facebook. One classmate lost her mother shortly before I lost Marie. We have been exchanging texts and phone calls for a little over a month. Tomorrow, we are going on our second date. By the way, she has been living in Florida.

January 31, 2015
Teaching
I don't think I could have picked a better profession to be in while grieving. Most of my substituting is done at the elementary level. Kids that age are "people pleasers." They want to make you happy so that you will like them. Also, at that age, they are curious, happy, and energetic. Whatever my mood, being surrounded by kids lifts my spirits. I even enjoy cafeteria duty.

Yesterday, I realized how a school could be a metaphor for grief. I was standing in the hallway before the students arrived and I marveled at how quiet and lifeless the school felt. As time went by, children started showing up. At first just one or two at a time, then, as the buses arrived, ten or 20 at a time. Soon, the building was noisy and full of life, as it should be.

Early stages of grief feel quiet and lifeless. Over time, little patches of sunlight and joy sneak in. As more time passes, full Sun light and happiness returns. Life begins again, as it should. By the way, the second date went very well, thank you.

Cynthia was living in Florida. When her mother died, she was named executrix and was staying at her mom's house, getting it ready to sell. Her siblings turned off the cable and wi-fi to save costs. When Cynthia told me her situation, I offered her a room at my house, as I had three bedrooms I wasn't using. At this point we were just friends and I was trying to help.

The more time we spent with each other, the more I knew I wanted to be more than friends. One night, we came home from having dinner. We sat in the car in the driveway listening to a Tim McGraw CD. He sang, "One of these days you're going to love me." I began to sing along. It was very romantic. I think that was when she began feeling the same way I did.

We kissed. There was nothing awkward about it. We were two lonely people who had found a second chance for love. We were both happy, and still are.

February 1, 2015
Don't Go It Alone
A friend to rely on
A shoulder to cry on
Share your grief
Don't go it alone
If you share
Someone will care

If you are hurting
Pick up the phone
Don't sit in your room
Surrounded by gloom
No one wants to
See you sit and moan
It has been quite a while
Since I have seen you smile
Go out and sing
It's time to change your tone
Your life did not end
Time to call a friend
Cry on their shoulder
Just don't go it alone

February 2, 2015
I Can't Have Anything Nice
That was a favorite saying of Marie's. A deer would run into her car, causing damage, and she would say, "I can't have anything nice." She would break a dish and say, "I can't have anything nice."

Time and time again, I would point out the many ways that we had been blessed. She stuck to her mantra.

I, being the eternal optimist, could never relate. Though devastated by her death, I refuse pity myself. My life goes on. There is work to do, bills to pay. Though I know I am not through mourning, there is new joy in my life. I can have something nice.

February 3, 2015
Dead
You probably noticed my posts have been a little more upbeat. The sun came out again and so on.

I have also said that I am aware that I am not done mourning. It's good to be a realist. Optimism is great (I highly recommend it) but you have to be prepared for down times as well. Today, I started a three-day assignment -- three days in the same classroom! My first class was spelling. I had to deliver a spelling test.

I would read a word, use it in a sentence, then read the word again. I should have read the list before class. All was going well until I reached the last word: dead.

I read it and said, "Dead."
I thought, "My wife is dead."
I repeated, "Dead." One student asked if I was going to use it in a sentence. I slowly shook my head no as I fought back tears. Grief, I am finding, is somewhat like Candid Camera. Someday, when you least expect it, someone will walk up to you and say, "Cry! Your wife is dead."

February4, 2015
We're All In This Together
Today, in class, we were reading "Because of Winn-Dixie," a young adult novel. The study guide said that characters Otis and Opal were both lonely and that in class, students should write about a time they were lonely.

One boy said he has never been lonely. Then he asked me if I have been lonely.

I told him I was lonely when my wife died. It got very quiet in the room.

Then I said that was why I enjoyed teaching so much. I get to spend time with young, happy people. I smiled to reassure them that I was okay. Another line in the book was, "I believe, sometimes that the whole world has an aching heart."

I know I've addressed this before however I need to remind myself that I am not alone in my grief. Death, divorce, separation or some other sad experience touches everyone. I need to work on being more empathetic and more sensitive to other people's pain. Being able to console someone else in their hour of grief may be just the right medicine to help heal my heartache.

February 5, 2015
Darkness/Dawn
I received an invitation to join a grief support group. I already belong to two grief support groups: my church and Facebook. There was a poem included in the invitation that I think is worth sharing:

"What to Do in Darkness" by Marilyn Chandler McEntire
Go slowly
Consent to it
But don't wallow in it
Know it as a place of germination
And growth
Remember the light
Take an outstretched hand if you find one
Exercise unused senses
Find the path by walking it
Practice trust
Watch for the dawn

This has been my journey. I have acknowledged grief, but I have not wallowed in it. I took time to recall happy memories. I took hold of an outstretched hand and am finding the dawn. In the depth of my darkness, a beautiful ray of sunshine has entered my life and I am, once again, a happy man.

Tomorrow would have been Marie's 57th birthday. I made a decision to not spend the day home alone. I will be going to State College with a friend to see some Penn State ice hockey and will not be posting again until Sunday.

February 8, 2015
You Can't Hide
Friday would have been Marie's 57th birthday. I was invited to go to Penn State and enjoy a couple of hockey games. Since 1974, I have considered Penn State my home.

I thought it would be a good idea to get out of my house and go have some fun, to avoid quiet reflective time on her birthday. What better place to spend it than Penn State?

It was a fun weekend. I got to spend time with my friend, my son, and my son's friends. We saw some great hockey and got to listen to a great band in a great bar. It was all good except for Facebook on my phone. I should have known better and left my phone at home.

Every time I looked at Facebook, another well-meaning, loving friend posted a comment about how much they missed Marie. There were many pictures of Marie in happier times.

Please don't misunderstand if you were one of the culprits. I really do appreciate that you are keeping her memory alive. The fault was all mine. I have said several times that you cannot hide from grief. It is better to face it and deal with it as it comes. I should have taken my own advice.

February 9, 2015
I'm Alright

Marie died. My world was turned upside down. I have been making adjustments. I am cooking healthy meals, doing laundry, cleaning, and paying bills. Add to that taking care of my dog, working, getting out to play once in a while, and reconnecting with old friends.

One of these friends happens to be a high school classmate who is also grieving. We met for dinner one night so that each of us could avoid being alone for a few hours. A few phone calls and many texts later, our relationship is blossoming. We will be going to a concert on Friday and she will be accompanying me to the karaoke party on Saturday.

Marie is still in my thoughts and my heart and always will be. However, the darkness is lifting and sunshine is returning to my life.

February 10, 2015
Alive
I woke up alive today
A gift from God again
My thanks I offer when I pray
Another chance to pick up a pen
To write about the way I feel
And help others by sharing
Poetry that helps me heal
And know others are caring
Another chance to smell a rose
To see a magnificent rainbow
And marvel at the life I chose
Decide where I will go
To share a meal with friends
Take a quiet walk with Lady
For all offences, make amends
Find a spot cool and shady

And have a quiet talk
To thank Him for my life
For allowing me to walk
For many years with my wife
Now she's gone, I know
The tears run down my face
And I wonder why she had to go
I trust she is in a better place

February 11, 2015
Friends
There is no "mourning manual," no set timeline, nothing that tells you when you've shed enough tears. Likewise, there is no manual on love, no set timeline, nothing that tells you who to fall in love with. Just like everything else in life, you deal with things as they come up, one day at a time, sometimes one hour at a time.

When you lose someone close to you, you cry, you deal with loneliness, you learn new routines. You may say goodbye to long loved traditions and hope to begin new traditions. Every day is a learning process. Through it all, you lean on God and your faith. You thank God for the support of family and friends, new and old. When new love enters your life, she is not replacing your lost loved one.

Think of it like a TV show where an actor leaves the show. The writers will sometimes "kill off" the departing character and write in a completely new character. The new actor does not replace the departed actor; he or she plays a completely new role. In life and love, you pray that family and friends will understand.

February 12, 2015
Raising a boy and a girl
Marie and Dave were giving life a whirl.
For many years
there were no tears.
And then Rascal Flatts sang about SaraBeth
the song reminded me of my wife's death.
Is it a crime
to make up for lost time?
There is a time to every season
Even when we don't know the reason.
A time to die
a time to cry

a time to ask why, why, why?
Amidst the grief
there is occasional relief.
A hug from a friend
and knowing that love does not end.
Dinner with a classmate
learning she is my soulmate.
Leaving friends torn
some want to warn
it is much too soon
to reach for the Moon.
Though I know in my heart
we will not part.
I hope and I pray
my new love and old friends will stay.

Apparently some people have an issue with my situation. I guess they think I should spend the rest of my life alone. I understand that they too, lost Marie and are still hurting. They are not the ones sitting alone in an empty house. They lost a friend. I lost my wife.

Let me ask you -- did you plan how, when, where, and with whom you were going to fall in love? Neither did I. It happened. I'm happy. I would hope that people who care about me would be happy for me.

Not one minute of one day goes by that I don't think about and dearly miss Marie. Nothing I can do will bring her back. I know many of you who knew her are still grieving. So am I. My feelings for the new person in my life do not detract from my feelings for Marie. I feel sorry for any of you who are willing to walk away from my friendship over this; however, it will be your loss.

February 13, 2015
The Vetting Process
Last night, we opened our home to two wonderful young people, PJ and Kristen, who are friends of my daughter and son-in-law. They are traveling and my daughter suggested they stay with us instead of at a hotel. I told my daughter that she was sending them on a recon mission to check up on their dad.

The four of us had a very enjoyable evening. I think Kristy and Lucas will get a positive report from their recon team. Tonight, we had dinner with Cynthia's daughter, son-in-law, and her daughter's friend. Once again, it was a very enjoyable evening.

Enjoyable that is, until we got to the Kuhnsville Hotel. The bartender must have been having a bad day because she was extremely rude to us. I explained to our group that I no longer wish to spend time with negative people, so we promptly left. Initial feedback is that I passed the test. I am looking forward to meeting more of her friends and family and introducing her to more of my friends and family.

February 14, 2015
Too soon?
As you know by now, I am dating a lady that I first met in 5th grade. Some concerned friends have cautioned that it is too soon for me to be romantically involved. A little history: When I was 16, I met a 14-year-old girl. That night, I told her that one day, I would marry her. We spent 42 years together, 36 as man and wife. I think I know my heart and I have done well trusting it in the past. I believe I will listen to my heart again.

February 15, 2015
Gumbo
Just as gumbo is a collection of random ingredients, today's post is a collection of random thoughts. We'll begin with last night. Cynthia and I attended a karaoke "prom." People dressed up, and the singers sang songs from their high school days. My date was looking good and having fun.

Throughout the evening, she danced with me, my brother, my friends, and other women. Near the end of the festivities, a woman approached me and told me my date was beautiful. I agreed. She then told me if I did not want her, she would take her. More amused than taken aback, I replied that I would keep her. She said, "Fine, be that way," shoved me and stormed away. Undeterred, the young lady offered my date a piece of paper with her name and number. My date politely declined.

After spending a week in this area visiting one daughter, Cyn is traveling west to visit another daughter. Once again, it will be me and my dog.

I will be doing schoolwork for my Reading Specialist course (first test on Wed.) and doing some quiet reflection. I will also be sending out letters of interest for five different teaching positions. After a long dry spell, it looks like some schools may be hiring next year.

When Marie was first diagnosed, she told me to find someone new. She told her friends that she did not wish for me to be alone. Is Cynthia "the one"? Only time will tell.

I do know that I am MUCH happier with her than I am when I am alone. Cynthia's friends and family who have met me, like me. My friends and family who have met Cyn, like her. So far, so good. At this point, 2015 is shaping up to be a much better year than 2014.

February 16, 2015
Living in a Fishbowl
I have been pouring my heart out for all the world to see for a little more than a month. There have been days of tears and days of joy, all of it shared with my Facebook friends and family. I started writing as a way to express and deal with my feelings of grief after the loss of my wife.

Throughout the process, I have received countless comments offering love and support. I have also been told that my posts have helped other people come to terms with their own feelings of grief. Recently, as you all know by now, I have found a new love. My posts have been documenting the turn from grief to joy.

In the process, we lost one friend who, unbeknownst to us, also had feelings for Cyn. Hopefully, in time, he will come to his senses and resume our friendship. [He never did; his loss.]

I am also hopeful that you and I will keep Marie's memory alive by sharing pictures, recipes, or happy stories. I would also hope that you will also find room in your hearts to accept Cyn and to be happy that we are happy together.

Marie and I were Baby Boomers, both born before Sputnik was launched. We grew up with three channels on black and white TV. We had dial telephones -- one per house. It was in the dining room or living room, plugged into the wall. There were no private phone calls unless you were home alone. There were no cell phones, computers, video games, or fidget spinners.

"OMG," say the youngsters. How did we survive?

We read books, played outside, and talked to each other. Summertime meant riding bikes and cooling off by spraying each other with a hose. We went bowling or roller skating. We watched the first moon landing on TV. We bit our knuckles over the Apollo 13 mission. We watched the Vietnam war on TV every night. We watched cities burn in the summer of 1968. As a freshman in college, I watched Nixon's resignation speech. While watching *Monday Night Football*, I learned of John Lennon's death. Marie was pregnant with Kristy at the time.

We marveled at the pace of technology. Some new wonder would be introduced only to become obsolete in less than a year. Obviously, there was no such thing as Facebook. I was an adult when it was introduced. I do not recall (to quote Ronald Reagan) how or when I found out about Facebook, I just know I was immediately hooked. I became a daily user right from the start. I was accepting friend requests from people I barely knew or didn't know at all.

For the most part, I used it as a political soapbox to promote and defend my conservative philosophy. That changed (temporarily) when Marie got sick. I used Facebook as a way to communicate with family and friends. It saved me from making dozens of painful calls. The few times I tried to make phone calls, I ended up in tears, unable to communicate.

I will probably remain a daily user of Facebook as long as I (and Facebook) am around. Marie never took an interest in it and never opened a page for herself. I guess she was too busy living her life to bother with it.

February 17, 2015
God Is Still Speaking
I like a TV show called *The Mentalist*. I don't always get to watch it when it is on, so I DVR it. Last night, I watched a taped episode from a few weeks ago. The lead character is Patrick Jane. His wife was murdered several years ago but he still loves her and still wears his ring. He is now dating his co-worker.

On this episode, he meets an old friend who mentions Jane's new love interest. He said, "You should have someone Patrick, you deserve to be happy."

Maybe it's time to take the ring off. No shame in moving on. Angela would want you to." Marie told me to find someone new. She told friends that she did not want me to be alone. That was so Marie, caring more about me than herself even in the midst of her illness. While I am seeing someone and "moving on," I am still wearing her ring. I will probably wear it the rest of my life.

February 18, 2015
Orion

Orion is my favorite constellation. It is easy to find on cold winter nights. He's an archer, just like my astrological sign, Sagittarius. He shows up every winter and leaves in spring. After Marie's death, a friend bought a star and had it named for her. I'm not sure where that star is but, for me, Marie is one of the stars in Orion.

She was born in the winter, we met in the winter, and she left us in the winter (actually late fall but Orion had already made his appearance). Also, when I walk Lady, Orion is directly over the house where Marie grew up. When I look at Orion, I know that Marie is up there, in Heaven. She is in a beautiful room, prepared for her by God. The room is full of flowers, puppies, and love.

See, Marie? You can have something nice. Take care of her, Orion.

P.S. I wrote this during a prep period today. Soon after I finished writing, a student came in to practice her flute. Her song choice? "Twinkle, Twinkle, Little Star." Cue the tears.

February 19, 2015
People come and people go
some you will get to know
Some will become your friend
and will be there until the end
Others are simply passing through
they will never really get to know you
Every once in a while
someone will give you a smile
A few will hold your hand
as you walk the land
With one or two you will fall in love
you will fit like a hand in a glove
She will find her way into your heart
so you will never want to part
You two will find a special song
that tells you you belong
You will wish upon a star
that from you she doesn't travel far
You will find the Sun
and know that she is the One.

<u>February 20, 2015</u>
CCCCOLD!!!!
I am not posting anything today because my fingers are frozen, the keys on my keyboard are frozen, my brain is frozen, my house is freezing, the roads are frozen. This is just stupid cold. My dog is asking me to teach her how to use the toilet so she doesn't have to pee outside. Where is this global warming I keep hearing about? Help!!!! I need to go somewhere where the only thing that is frozen is the margaritas.

<u>February 21, 2015</u>
Someday
When we retire, we're going to...
When we have enough money, we're going to...
When the kids are grown, we're going to...
When I get a better job, we're going to...
When we get the college loans paid off, we're going to...
When it's safer to travel in the Middle East, we're going to...
Someday, someday, someday...
If you are in love, tell her...now
If you want to see Yellowstone, go...now
If you want to sky dive, jump...now
If you have kids, tell them you love them...now
If you hate your job, find a new one...now
If you want to go back to school, start...now
No one is guaranteed tomorrow, the person you love may not be here tomorrow, you may not be here tomorrow.
Every day is a gift, every day is precious.
Time is your most precious possession.
If someone steals your money, you can get more money.
If your house burns down, you can build a new one.
Time lost is lost. You don't get a second chance at yesterday.
Today, live, laugh, love.

<u>February 22, 2015</u>
Imagine a life without any strife
A body without pain, a world without rain
No more fears, no more tears
No one crying, no one dying
Goodbye to the mess, goodbye to the stress
Would we be okay, should come that day
Strife and pain make us stronger
Rain makes crops grow longer

Crying releases toxins, dying ends suffering
I have found our trials eventually lead to smiles
Our joy is higher after surviving the fire

How can we know true joy without experiencing sadness? People don't appreciate rain until they live through a drought. When we struggle, we learn coping skills. We also learn to treasure family, friends, and time. The contrast between happy and sad colors our world. What a dull, boring, gray world it would be if all our needs were met, never having to struggle.

What sounds really good on paper may be a nightmare in practice. When you see rain, think of the flowers that will soon bloom. If you lose your job, think of the opportunities ahead. After surgery, focus on returning to health and strength. When you lose someone you love, grieve. As you grieve, remember that their life ended, yours did not. Know that one day, the sun will return and you will smile again.

February 23, 2015
Some good, some bad.
Some happy, some sad.
We don't know the reason
but events are the season
in your life.
Without strife, you would not know peace.
It may take years of tears to really find joy.
Today's pain will tomorrow mean sweet relief.
Grief will give way to laughter and smiles.
A journey of many miles
could be kind of boring.
Potholes, flat tires, and hitchhikers add to the stories
you'll tell to your friends.
No one shares tales of the miles of smooth roads.
They talk of the missed exits, detours, and unbearable loads.
When all is dark and life is kicking your ass,
Smile, and say, "This too shall pass."

February 24, 2015
Photographs and Memories
When all is said and done
each of us will live on
in photographs and memories.
Friends and family will talk

remember how we used to walk
along the shore of the beautiful seas?
Pictures will make us smile, laugh, or cry
then we will stop and ask why
did she have to leave us so soon?
We met while skating
and quickly began dating
soon after Neil first walked on the Moon.
We were young and in love
and when push came to shove
we just did as we please.
Now, my soul is bereft
for I have nothing left
except photographs and memories.

February 25, 2015
Spelling Lists
You're cruising along, everything is fine. You haven't cried in a
few days. You look at her picture, cherishing fond memories. You
go about your life, finding a new normal, without her and yet with
her, always. You never know when, where, or what will remind
you of her. Something always does, as I said before, when you
least expect it.

Today, it was the dreaded spelling list, again. A seemingly
innocuous word: haven't. I was reading the words for the test,
making a sentence, and rereading the word. Word number 8 --
"haven't" -- got me.

Early in Marie's battle, she chose as her inspiration, "white lights
pouring down from the heavens." Anyone from my generation
will recognize the lyrics from the Carly Simon song, "Haven't got
time for the pain."

I read the word, hesitated, said, "Haven't got time for the pain,"
hesitated, and repeated the word as a single tear trickled down my
cheek. Thankfully, the students were engaged in their work and
did not notice. One day at a time. One spelling list at a time.

February 26, 2015
You never think will come the day
When the one you love is taken away
You think your lovely bride
Will always walk by your side

You firmly believe
She will never leave
We'll grow old in our rocking chairs
Happy, without any cares
Then life plays a trick
And she gets very sick
The doctors confer
And say, "We can treat her."
They give her shots
And aim radiation at dots
But it is all just talk
Now she can no longer walk
Try as they might
The end is in sight
No cure can we gain
Only manage the pain
We say our goodbyes
As she closes her eyes
Comes that sad day
When she just slips away
And leaves me in tears
To face all my fears
Down on my knee
Alone as can be

February 27, 2015
Life is not fair
I ball my fist and punch the air
I wonder why
The good ones die
At an early age
When they've barely taken the stage
They leave the Earth
Too soon after birth
When the Devil's son
Charlie Manson
Is still here
Still invoking fear
It's a joke
That some people smoke
Two packs a day
And grow old anyway
Others drink like fish
Yet get another birthday wish

They ride motorcycles without protecting their head
And they are still not dead
Marie never took a chance
Around trouble she would dance
And still in the end
I lost my best friend
I just sit and stare
Saying life isn't fair

February 28, 2015
Some dis, some dat
Some good, some bad
Some happy, some sad
Some ups, some downs
Some smiles, some frowns
Sometimes you win, sometimes you lose
What you feel is what you choose
It's called life
Remember, you always appreciate a sunny day
more after a rainstorm came your way.

March 1, 2015
Tick tock, tick tock
The only sound comes from the clock
I am told
Nights are cold
When you are lonely
When you are the only
One in the bed
With only memories in your head
You reach out
You want to shout
Where have you gone
What have you done
No matter how hard you try
You can't help but cry
With no words left to say
She slipped quietly away
She did nothing to deserve the disease
Now I hope she is resting in peace

March 2, 2015
Love Math
Love. It doesn't follow any rules. If you and a friend have a candy
bar and want to share it, you each get 1/2 of the candy. If you
have a pizza and 2 friends, you each get 1/3 of the pizza.

When your wife gives birth to your first child, you love that child
with all your heart. When your wife gives birth to your second
child, you love that child with all your heart. Love isn't cut in half
and shared like candy; it is doubled.

The same is true when your wife takes her place in heaven. You
still love her with all your heart and will forever. When you find a
new love, you love her with all your heart, without diminishing the
love you have for your angel. Love is not a whole item that can be
cut and doled out in fractions. It is an eternal well with enough for
everyone. Everyone that you love gets all of your love. Love is the
only thing I know that can be doubled by sharing.

March 3, 2015
God puts us where he needs us. There are examples of this
throughout the Bible: Jonah, Moses, and the lamb when Abraham
was about to sacrifice Isaac come to mind. It can be something
simple like being in a grocery store aisle when a short, elderly lady
can't reach an item on the top shelf. It could be taking a new route
home and seeing a house on fire. Or it could be simply being
there for a friend.

I'm starting to believe that God also, on occasion, shields you.
When Marie was pregnant with my son, she continued to work in
spite of doctor's orders to rest. She was hospitalized and forced to
rest. The waiting game was on. Day after day, night after night, I
was driving to and from the hospital. One night, fiends invited me
to dinner. While we were eating, Marie had a seizure and an
emergency C section to deliver Brad.

Fast forward 25 years. Marie is bedridden due to her cancer. We
know she is going to die in the next week or so. I left to get a
haircut. On the way home, I turned around and went back to the
grocery store. Marie died when I was at the store.

Naturally, I have spent some time beating myself up about not
being there for her at these crucial moments. A very good friend

gave me a different perspective. She asked me if maybe God did not want me to have these painful memories of Marie. Maybe he wanted to protect me and pulled me away at just the right moment.

Our God is an awesome and loving God and He has blessed me with some awesome and loving friends.

March 4, 2015
Protocol
When you lose your spouse, how long should you wait before you go on a date? When you date someone, how long should you wait to introduce them to your family? When should they meet your friends? I can't seem to find a rule book for any of this. So, like life in general, I'm making it up as I go along.

Cynthia has introduced me to her daughters, her son-in-law, and her grandson. I like them and they seem to approve of me. Cynthia has met several of my friends, members of my church family, two of my brothers, and my mother (who is very happy for me). She received thumbs-up from everyone.

We have not gotten together with three of the most important people in my life: my son, my daughter, and my son-in-law. We're hoping to remedy that situation in the next couple of weeks. Meanwhile, if someone finds that book with all the rules, keep it. I think I'm doing okay without it.

March 5, 2015
Winter
White everywhere
Inside all the time
No end in sight
Take me to Florida
Everyone is complaining
Really? More snow?
Why?
I can't take any more.
No more snow!
Time for Spring
Each new storm
Raises my blood pressure.
What the heck
is going on?

Not fit for human habitation
Think spring
Even skiers have had enough
Rethinking Pennsylvania.
Wahhhh!
It's Not The Inevitable Reality.

I quit. Fire the weatherman. I'm taking a sledgehammer to my snow blower. I'm going to spray paint the snow in my yard green. I'm going to put sand on the bathroom floor, fill the tub with water, put on some Jimmy Buffett, and pretend I'm at the beach. And, when it does warm up, I will not complain about how hot it is.

I feel better now.

March 6, 2015
Short or Long?
Chris Rock says that life isn't short; it's long, and you have to live with the choices you make. I say it is all about perspective. If you did something dumb and are spending 10 years in prison, life is long. If you are with someone you love, working a job you love and are told you have ten years to live, life is short.

Picture the person you fantasize about. You have three minutes to make love with them. Life is short. You have to sit naked on a block of ice for three minutes. Life is long. You are in the middle of your work week. Life is long. Your are in the middle of your vacation week. Life is short. It is March and it has been snowing since October. Life is long. School is out in mid-June and starts again in late August. Life is short.

Your life partner leaves before you realized your dream of becoming a teacher. She leaves before you have grandchildren. She leaves before you get to enjoy retirement together. She leaves before you get to spend your children's inheritance. Please don't tell me life is long. Life is short. Treasure each day. If you are with someone you love, tell them, now. Life is short. Live, laugh, love.

March 7, 2015
Lonely we are not meant to be
That is very obvious to me
If we were supposed to be alone
We would have no need for a phone

We would not need a place for singles to meet
Movie theaters would have only one seat
There would be no baseball or football
Golf would be no fun at all
With no hand to hold
Life would be so cold
No joys or sorrows to share
When you hurt, no one would care
There would be no we
Just lonely you and me
That is not Life
Man needs a wife
As we go on this walk
We need someone to talk
Loneliness is a cage
Against its bars I rage
If I am to live
If I still have more to give
There has to be two
I need someone to talk to
Lonely we are not meant to be

March 8, 2015
Without Marie
Am I still me
It was always Marie and Dave
Two seats they would save
Now one is empty
Am I still me
Married or single
Am I allowed to mingle
I look in the mirror to see
Am I still me
When friends I meet
Out on the street
They want to flee
Am I still me
Our house is a lonely place
When her face
Only in pictures I see
Am I still me
Now alone I stand
In this uncertain land
Someone hear my plea

Am I still me
How will I know
Where I should go
Without Marie
Am I still me

When you lose your partner of 40 years, you lose a part of your identity. All of our friends were married couples. Get-togethers were always even numbers. Now, instead of being a part of a couple, I am alone, the odd one out. People are trying to figure out what to do with just Dave.

I am trying to figure out where I fit, trying to adjust to a new reality. Places that used to be warm and comforting now seem foreign and cold. I did not just lose my wife; I lost my place in the community. I feel like I no longer belong.

I don't blame anyone. Maybe it's my perception being warped by trauma. I just have this strong feeling that it is time for a fresh start somewhere else, where they did not know Marie. I need to go somewhere that I can learn to be just Dave.

March 9, 2015
Layers
It snows a couple of inches. The temperature drops and a hard crust forms on top of the soft snow. It snows again and the process is repeated. After many snowy, cold months, you walk on top of many layers of snow. Hard, soft, hard, soft. You feel like you are walking on solid ground, however you are actually more than a foot off the ground.

As you walk, you occasionally hit a weak spot and your foot breaks through the crust. You sink into soft snow beneath, sometimes one layer and sometimes several layers. Walking is treacherous. A twisted ankle or a torn ACL is always one step away. You keep hoping for a spring thaw and safer conditions, but it is slow in coming.

Grief is like that. You go through each day, everything going smoothly. You hear a favorite song and feel a twinge of sadness. You see a picture and think of unfulfilled dreams. You break through the second layer and a tear appears. You look at the calendar and see a birthday, anniversary, or a holiday and break down right to the ground. Tears flow.

How long until spring? When will the tears stop? Family, friends, and faith ease the journey. It is a journey without a map or a timetable. All I ask is that you walk with me a ways. And, if you see me shed a tear, offer me a shoulder.

<u>March 10, 2015</u>
Books
Every book has a beginning, a middle, and an end. The beginning has to grab your attention, make you empathize with the characters, and make you want to keep reading. The middle is where the action takes place. Some books are exciting page turners that keep you reading late into the night. Others slow down or get confusing and make reading each page a chore. The end is where there is resolution. The problems are solved and the mysteries unraveled. Some endings are happy, some sad. Sometimes you are glad to be done reading the book; other times you don't want it to ever end.

People's lives also have beginnings, middles, and ends. They are born, they live their lives, they die. Unlike books, though, the beginning of one life is in the middle or end of other lives. The middle includes beginnings, middles, and ends of other lives.

As one person dies, babies are being born, people are living their lives, and others are also dying. Life can be like a book in another way as well. When you finish a good book, you talk about it with your fellow readers. You may share the book so others will also find joy in its pages. So many books "live on" long after they were first published; To Kill a Mockingbird, Gone With the Wind, Treasure Island, Insert the title of your favorite book here…

People, after they die, will be remembered by family and friends. Stories will be shared.
"Remember the way Marie..."
"OOOH the cookies Marie made…"
"She always took time to..."
Like a great book, Marie will be remembered and talked about for a very long time.

I subbed for a 6th grade class today. The teacher notes said that if the students get their work done, reward them with a trip to the gym. They got the work done, so we went to the gym.

One boy was like Magic Johnson, hitting shots consistently from the three-point line. I threw a few balls that came close to hitting the backboard. At the end of class, the boy said, "Teach, you suck… at basketball. Why you suck so bad at ball?"
I said, "I'm white and white guys can't shoot hoops."
A girl said, "That's not it. You suck at it 'cause you're old."
Kids crack me up.

March 11, 2015
The Forest
Imagine being in a forest. It is morning and the sunrise is beautiful. You are with your best friend and have all the gear and supplies you need for several days. You have no obligations except to enjoy the scenery and companionship. Life is good!

Imagine, now, the same forest. Now the sun is setting. You are alone and have no gear or food. Losing a spouse is kind of like that. One day, life is good. The world is at your command. All you have to do is live, breathe, and enjoy.

Then, suddenly, everything changes. Now you are alone in a cold, unfriendly, unknown place. You have no map and no guide. The future that once looked rosy now is gray and scary. There are a few individuals who like being alone. I am not one of them.

March 12, 2015
Is there a God?
Because I know there is, I am called close-minded. Is there a heaven? If there is a God, there must be a heaven. Is Marie in heaven? I know she is. She is probably baking cookies for God and Jesus. She is probably surrounded by puppies that never grow old. She probably lives in a mansion that looks over a lake. She is probably with her mom and dad. She is probably smiling, happy that I listened to her and found someone new.

March 13, 2015
Middle
I am serving as building substitute for Broughal Middle School. It is situated, appropriately, in between the once-powerful and now defunct Bethlehem Steel and the prestigious Lehigh University.

In the middle, on one side: gritty, dirty, death, a dismal life of hard work, or no work, leading nowhere. On the other side: vibrant, life full of hope for the future and opportunity. Some students will go one way and end up on welfare or in jail, tied to the past. Others will excel and move on to college and bright futures. Some will make choices, good or bad, and some will drift with the crowd and have decisions made for them.

You can't live in the middle. You can't stay the same. As Joe Paterno said, "If you're not getting better, you're getting worse."

Life is like that. On one side is grief and despair, and on the other, hope and happiness. Where you live is not dictated by circumstance but by choice. Your choice. I choose happiness. Live, laugh, love... and tonight I will add: sing.

March 14, 2015
My life is not the same without my wife.
We had it made, or so I thought.
We'll pay off the house and travel.
We'll get together with friends and family.
We'll donate our time to worthy charities.
Or, she'll check out early.
Leave me broken and confused.
Don't get me wrong, I don't blame her.
It was the cancer that screwed up our plans.
One day, we'll find a cure.
We'll stop that hateful disease dead in its tracks.
Until then, I'm left to carry on.
I'll find my way, even smile again, someday.

March 15, 2015
I Wish
I wish she could come back
Even if for just one day
I know I would not lack
For things I want to say
"Sorry" would be my first word
I love you would soon follow
My angel would fly like a bird
And swoop with joy like a swallow
It would not change my plight
The next day I would still be alone
But I would try to make things right
For all my faults, try to atone
In my words maybe she would find
Even when I was selfish

She was always on my mind
Just one more day, I wish

March 16, 2015
Sometimes I have to really try
not to cry
When I am in school
it would not be cool
to let my emotions show.
When I tell students that my wife died
they all just want to hide.
They can't relate to my pain.
Sometimes grief is like a chain
tying me down, you know?
She is in my head and in my heart
days go by, I don't know where to start.
She left me in November
and now I try to remember
the scent of her hair.
The Lord took her home
and now I am alone.
But I will start over again
with the help a very close friend.
We just have to decide where.

March 17, 2015
Blue Skies
Temperatures rise under blue sunny skies
Snow begins to melt the cold that you felt
all winter long becomes a memory
Grass reappears as summertime nears
Robins return and their babies learn
how to fly under their parents' watchful eye
Flowers bloom as you walk in the room
Where last year you held her near
celebrating the years you spent together
Her kiss yesterday's bliss
forever gone and yet I live on
picking up pieces of shattered dreams
Will I reach my goal to teach?
The dream we dared the dream we shared
Lord, take me where you need me.

<u>March 18, 2015</u>
Black and White
Some people live in a black-and-white world. Events and people
are good or bad. There are calamitous disasters or joyous
celebrations, evil people and virtuous people. No in-between.

I live in a grey world. People are people. Good people do bad
things and bad people do good things. Robin Hood was a thief,
but he gave what he took to the poor. Dr. House was an amazing
diagnostician but he was a nasty, sarcastic drug addict. Forest fires
are destructive, yet they clear the way for new life. Floods destroy
homes and take lives, but they leave rich topsoil that allows lush
new growth. Death is painful for friends and relatives, however, it
ends suffering and begins eternal heavenly life.

Grief can be all consuming, if that is your choice. You can live in
your black-and-white world, sit in a corner, and cry. Or you can
live in a grey world where grief and joy co-exist. You can mourn
the passing of a loved one while embracing new love. Loving
someone new does not detract from your first love. Mourning
your late wife does not prevent you from loving someone new
with all your heart. Welcome to my world. Live, laugh, love.

I have not had any inspired thoughts in a while so I have not
posted anything in the last few days. Today, I forced myself to sit
down and write something. After all, I did promise to post daily
for a year, and here I was slacking after only a couple of months.

I had only one thought in my mind: mirror. By the time I was
done, I was in tears. Enjoy. Hopefully, I'll be back tomorrow.

<u>March 19, 2015</u>
I'm back as promised. I woke up and went about living my life.
I'm still trying to make sense of everything. Still trying to figure
out what I am supposed to do and where I am supposed to go. I
won't say we had it all planned out. We were too busy living our
lives to really sit down and plan.

Big events force you to sit down and think, "What now?" A fire,
flood, or hurricane might destroy your home. Loss of a job, birth
of a child, or a death of a loved one will force you to sit down
and think. Most days, most of us just go through the motions of
daily life without a thought about tomorrow. I'm not saying that's

wrong. That's life. And I'm not saying we should worry about tomorrow. I guess I'm saying we might be better prepared if we, every once in a while, sat down and thought about tomorrow. Maybe discuss things like what we would we do if…

<u>March 20, 2015</u>
The Ocean
Have you been to the beach? There's nothing like digging your toes into the sand, especially if you've been dealing with snow for months. Usually, the ocean is predictable and calming. The clock-like tides and waves lapping against the beach mesmerize you.

Every once in a while, though, a hurricane comes ashore. The winds tear down houses and piers and the water pushes sand all over the place. It can take months or years for a shore town to recover. Life and grief can be like that. Everything settled into a dull routine of working and paying bills -- until…

<u>March 21, 2015</u>
The Curtain
Down come salty tears
When thoughts of the future
Give birth to fears
She's gone to her rest
I pray that her soul
Will be blessed
Now I must go on
Somehow, knowing
That she's gone
What will be my life
After so many years
With her as my wife
She was my bride
All through life
We walked side by side
Will I still be able
To pay bills
And put food on the table
When the grieving ends
Who will be left
Of our many friends
So much is uncertain
If only we could
Peek behind the curtain

To look at tomorrow
And see an end
To today's sorrow

March 22, 2015
Another year gone by
Fifty two weeks
The days a wink of an eye
Swing sets and grade school
Are all in the past
Now I'm so cool
A high school grad
A little bit of college
Now I'm a Dad
Swing sets and skinned knees
And learning how to deal
With high school bullies
Look the kids have grown
We are so proud
Of the seeds we've sown
Marie and I
Can now enjoy
The Sun and the sky
Then Cancer came along
That wretched beast
Interrupted our song
She fought gallantly
Beating the Beast
Wasn't meant to be
Now I am left
To go on with my life
Totally bereft
Day after day
The wrinkles appear
And my hair turns gray
I know, my friend
My time is nearly
At its end
So I sit and ponder
What has happened
I wonder
How did so many years go by
In what seems
To be a wink of an eye

PART FOUR: SPRING

<u>March 23, 2015</u>
Mirror
I look in the mirror and see myself
Am I seeing the past or the future?
Am I looking ahead or looking back?
She's gone but she's right beside me
She's not here but she'll always be with me
Are Dave and Marie coming?
Let's invite Dave and Marie
Let's go see Dave and Marie
Now it's Just Dave
Marie did not want that
Before she left she said, "Find somebody new."
She was dying and all she thought about was me being alone
Have you met Cynthia
I hear she's nice
I think Dave and Cynthia are in love
Are Dave and Cynthia coming?
Let's invite Dave and Cynthia
Let's go see Dave and Cynthia
I look in the mirror and see myself
I am seeing Cynthia in my future
I am seeing Marie smiling

<u>March 24, 2015</u>
Directions
Fold flap A on to line B... Lather, rinse, repeat... Go to the
Kopper Penny and turn left...

A big part of education is learning how to follow directions.
Unfortunately, many of my students either don't know how or
refuse to follow directions. That, however is a topic for another
forum. The direction I am heading with this is that, although there
are directions everywhere to almost everything, there are no
directions on how to live your life.

Yes, there is the Bible, the Torah, and the Koran, among others, which give general directions. But I'm talking about specifics. What should I be when I grow up? With whom should I fall in love? As a parent, what should I do when my kid...?

You can talk to friends, clergy, and counselors, but for the most part, we are all just winging it. How long should I spend mourning? With whom should I share my pain and grief? I'm winging it.

Thankfully, I have some awesome friends and a strong faith to make the journey a little more bearable. If you happen upon me, wandering aimlessly, walk with me a ways and point me in the right direction.

March 25, 2015
Marie, Marie everywhere I look I see
things she touched, things she wore
More and more I wonder how long
I'll be singing her song
Gone, gone, no more tomorrow's
still dealing with yesterday's sorrows
Light, light the touch of her hand on mine
running my hand through her hair so fine
Live , live I want to live my life
even though I miss so much, my wife
Laugh, laugh how I yearn to once again laugh
though what I've lost was my better half
Love, love lost love and new love's promise
remembering Marie and our one last kiss

March 26, 2015
One man doing the best he can
Ever onward, ever forward
You'll never know why she had to fly
You can sit and cry or continue to try
It's your choice so find your own voice
You used to be two now you're just you
Don't you know? You've got to fly solo
Or find someone you met and start a new duet
Are you going to teach or sit on a beach
No matter what life will bring, I will continue to sing
I lost the best but I still feel blessed
I lost Marie but the Lord still loves me.

The fraternity house that I lived in at Penn State for three years has been condemned and torn down. I have a picture of it in my office. Joe Paterno coached at Penn State for 60 years. He was fired and, shortly thereafter, died from cancer. I have a picture of him in my office.

The elementary school I attended was turned into senior apartments several years ago. A friend of ours was a karaoke DJ. He died at a young age. His Facebook page is still up.

Marie is gone. Her picture is in my wallet. I see her every time I use my credit card.

Things change, people come and go. We are left with pictures, postcards, ticket stubs and other mementos.

In my mind, the fraternity still stands. In my mind when I drive past my old school, I see an elementary school, not apartments. In my mind, Joe is still prowling the sidelines at Penn State. In my mind, my friend is still handing me a mic; it's my turn to sing. In my mind, Marie is still here, by my side.

March 28, 2015
What do you value?
What is your treasure?
Is it here or up above?
Is it something you measure?
Or someone you love?
Can you see it, touch it, feel it?
Are you worried someone will steal it?
Is there more on your mind ?
Or is it one of a kind?
What deserves your care --
Diamonds and gold?
The smell of her hair?
Or a hand you can hold?
What do you desire?
Do you need piles of cash?
Is it a car you require?
What is in your stash?
Something I have learned

Since I've gotten old
My treasure can't be burned
I have no need for gold
Tick-tock, tick-tock
What I value
Is measured by a clock
If I only knew
The importance of time
Misspent time cannot be replaced
It should be a crime
Your time to waste
Seconds with friends
Minutes with your lover
When your life ends
You can never recover
Hours spent worrying
Days spent drunk
Weeks spent hurrying
To load stuff in your trunk
So when you look back on your years
I hope that you see
More smiles than tears
And the best things in life are free

March 29, 2015
Snow
Winter snow comes on hard and fast. Snow blankets the ground.
Everything changes. Driving is dangerous, so you stay home more
often. Animals hibernate.

It gets colder and more snow comes. Sometimes heavy snow is
predicted and very few flakes fall. Other times, they predict
flurries and we get buried in snow. It feels like forever since you
felt the warmth of the sun. It starts to feel like a permanent
situation, that winter will not end. Then the days start to get
longer. The sun gets back to work. Temperatures rise and the
snow begins to melt. Green grass reappears and colorful flowers
start to bloom. Smiles return.

Then, out of nowhere, a spring blizzard pops up, dumping snow
and crushing spirits.

Spring eventually closes the door on winter, robins return and
outdoor life resumes.

Grief can be like that. At first, it is all consuming. Life stops. You are told to not make any important decisions. At times, you feel like the pain will never end. It can be unpredictable. You may approach a situation thinking that tears are a certainty and somehow you get through it. Other times, out of nowhere, tears flow and you are brought to your knees.

Eventually, you adjust to a new normal. Then one day, you look at a picture, you hear a song on the radio, or you simply have a gentle whisper of a memory and the pain and tears return.

I have faith that summer is coming.

March 30, 2015
I am facing the reality
And seeing my own mortality
Though I don't know why
We all have to die
I know at this stage
I'm past middle age
My mind says I'm seven
But I'm closer to Heaven
I could sit around and cry
Knowing I'm going to die
But if I am to survive
I want to be fully alive
I want to see every sight
And watch the stars at night
I want to dance and sing
I want to do everything
I hope you know
That when I go
I will have done quite a lot
And my body will be completely shot

March 31, 2015
With Hope
Blue moon hoping soon
to see my Marie
Big heart so smart
She left I wept
Stormy skies teary eyes
New life no wife

Big home all alone
In school I'm cool
Why cry I try
Go on Stay strong
Spring's here brings cheer
with hope I cope

April 1, 2015
Cyn
In the depths of my despair
I met a girl with bi-color hair
A heart like hers is something rare
that I should Love her is only fair
In a Winter cold as ice
I really needed something nice
She came into my life
not replacing my wife
but opening a new chapter
of love ever after
Where haven't you been
my world traveling Cyn?
All I ask, whatever you do
from now on, take me with you.
Live, laugh, Love!

April 2, 2015
Runaway Train
It hit me like a train
my tears falling like rain
wandering the halls
trapped inside these walls
I want to yell
shout "Go to Hell!"
maybe get some relief
from my consuming grief
months have past
how long will the pain last
I have really tried
very hard to hide
my tears from the kids
who hide under their lids
sometimes my eyes give me away
there is nothing left to say
let it rain

April 3, 2015
My dear Marie
Now, at last, you are free
You beat the cancer
Fire was your answer
You are no longer in pain
Our loss is Heaven's gain
You watch over us now
God's loving hand on your brow
You are in a room up above
Surrounded by Love
You are gone
We are left to go on
With tears flowing free
Making it hard to see
That smiles will return
On some future morn

April 4, 2015
Every Sunday, I go to church, as I have for many years. Every Sunday, we say the Apostles' Creed. At the end of the Creed, we state our beliefs: "I believe in the Holy Spirit, the holy catholic church, the communion of saints, the forgiveness of sins, the resurrection of the body,
and the life everlasting. Amen."

We don't need to read it. We know the words. We've been saying them every week for 50 years. The question is, when the rubber hits the road, do we believe the words?

That question was posed to me by my former pastor when Marie and I lost her mom. Resurrection? Life everlasting? Can we even wrap our heads around those concepts? There is no proof. The only way to find out if the words are true is to die, leaving no way to come back and report the findings.

There is only one answer. It is a one word answer: Faith. Faith is believing what you can't see, touch, hear, or prove. I have that faith. I believe that Marie and all those we have loved and lost are in heaven waiting for us. I believe that she exists in a place without sorrow or pain and that she is in the presence of God. This faith is what allows me to go on, to live my life, to smile again.

<u>April 5, 2015</u>
Easter
I was warned that holidays would be difficult. I have been settling in to new routines and trying to develop a new normal. Things were going pretty well. I was smiling again and making plans for a busy summer. Two days ago, it hit me that for the first time in 42 years Marie would not be with me for Easter. When I say it hit me, I mean it hit me, hard -- tears flowing and gasping for breath. I had to fight to regain composure throughout the last three days.

Cyn has been a great comfort to me as, hopefully I have been to her. She lost her mother shortly before Marie left us and has also been dealing with leaky eyes. We both take comfort in knowing that our loved ones are in God's loving arms and in the Easter message of forgiveness. Happy Easter, everyone.

Marie's second favorite holiday was Easter. Weeks before, she would begin decorating. She would give me a rare, childlike grin and say, "The bunnies are coming, the bunnies are coming!"

Indeed, by Easter, there were bunnies throughout the house. One Easter tradition we began when our children were little was to make a bunny cake. We would make two circular cakes. One would be the bunny's face; the other would be cut to make ears and a bow tie. After frosting, we applied coconut fur, jelly-bean eyes, and Twizzler whiskers. Even as adults, our children expected the bunny cake on Easter.

Another tradition was the Easter egg hunt in our yard. I would hide colored plastic eggs in trees, bushes, and in plain sight. Adults and children would scramble to find the most eggs. Marie never participated. She took pleasure in watching others enjoy themselves.

<u>April 6, 2015</u>
Fifty-six
Marie, she left way too soon.
Work and save, work and save.
Can't spend the money we make.
We're going to need it when we're old.
Then we will travel, then we will go.
We'll get into our motorhome and drive
And we'll see this great country.
Someday, we'll do it if we're still alive.

When I was about a year old, I became very sick. When my temperature reached 104, my parents drove me to the hospital. I stopped breathing on the way. My father had been a lifeguard at Kennywood pool

100

in Pittsburgh, so he knew how to do CPR. He gave me mouth-to-mouth respiration while my mom drove. After several days, the fever broke and I went home. It was not my time.

One summer day, when Marie was a little girl, she was playing in the meadow near her home. In the meadow was a pond. Though she did not know how to swim, the cool water was irresistible on that hot day. She wandered in and soon was in over her head and in trouble. Fortunately, her brother saw her, jumped in and pulled her out. It was not her time.

When I was in college, once a month, I would drive home for a weekend. I would go from State College to Marie's house in Bath, a three-hour trip. After spending a few hours, I would then drive to my parents' house 20 minutes away. Though I was tired, I always made it home okay.

There was one night when I was exceptionally tired. I was fighting to stay awake and apparently lost the fight two minutes from home. I fell asleep at the wheel at the top of a hill. I woke up a half mile later, on the wrong side of the road after having passed underneath a railroad trestle. Had another car been coming or if I had hit the concrete trestle, I could have been killed. It was not my time. I have never been a daredevil but I am also not ruled by fear. I know that one day, God will call me home. Until then, I will live my life without fear.

<u>April 7, 2015</u>
Spring
Spring sprung
Winter done
Warm sunny
See bunny
I'm happy
Sometimes sappy
No tear
This year
Scooter ride
Ocean tide
Students testing
Teachers resting
Robins nesting
Eggs hide
Smiles spied
Right here
No fear
Toes tapping
Afternoon napping
Life's funny

New honey
Cares flung
Summer's begun.

April 8, 2015
Live
My wife
she was my life
from our first date
our love was great
together so long
we shared a favorite song
one day she left
and I was bereft
I stare at the Moon
hoping I will see her again soon
please don't worry
I'm not really in a hurry
there's more living to be done
more races to be won
I really want to teach
young minds I want to reach
let me live
I still have much to give
looking forward to happier times
perhaps in warmer climes
I want to travel to a few more states
maybe go on a few more dates
I want my kids to see me grow old
there's more of this story to be told
with a little help from above
I will Live, Laugh, and Love.

April 9, 2015
The Dream
Big dreams
sometimes it seems
the world is yours
in spite of the pain
through the misty rain
you stay the course
eye on the goal
no matter the toll

you 'll get where you 're going
No time to rest
just give it your best
go forward never slowing
you just have to try
no time to cry
shout it out loud
I want to teach
this goal I will reach
to make Marie proud.

April 10, 2015
You all know people who complain, "I hate my job, my car is a
piece of crap, my house is a piece of junk"? For every one of
those people, there is someone looking at them saying, "I wish I
had a job, I wish I had a car, I wish I had a house."

While I have seen mansions and yachts and wondered how people
could afford those things, I have never envied them. I thank God
every day that I have a roof over my head and food in my belly.
You don't have to go far to find someone under a blanket on a
bench, their meager possessions in a trash bag. You don't have to
go far to find someone existing on one meal a day. I see these less
fortunate people and tell myself, "There, but for the grace of
God, go I."

I know that I am blessed. I also know I am obliged to share those
blessings. Some of my best days have been spent pounding nails,
doing plumbing, or painting in someone's storm-damaged home.
For many years, I have donated money to churches and charities. I
have done everything right and still, God took my wife.

Others in similar situations blame God for the cancer. They rage
at God and His churches. Others simply lose faith and stop
believing in God altogether.

Losing Marie hurt me deeply. It still hurts every day. I lost Marie,
many friends, and am estranged from some of my family. I am
still here. I still have things to accomplish. I am thankful for
friends who have remained by my side. I am confident that I will
make new friends. I am confident that God needs me, has a plan
for me.

Imagine you are on a roller coaster. In your car, there is a steering wheel. You can turn the wheel left, you can turn it right. Regardless of your efforts, the car is going to follow the tracks and take you to the final destination. I figured out a few years ago that I would enjoy the ride more if I just took my hands off the wheel.

My new prayer is very short: "Lord, You know what I need better than I do. Take me where you need me. Your will be done. Amen."

Life does go on. And life is better when you stop struggling and listen to God.

April 11, 2015
I don't know if you have ever taken on a monumental task. I did not start out intending to write a book, although I have had several false starts before. I started two different children's books and one science fiction book. All three efforts stalled after just a few pages. This project is different.

It is different in several ways. First, it did not start out as a book. It started as Facebook posts that helped me deal with my grief. Secondly, it comes from my heart. Any good writer or writing teacher will tell you, "Write what you know." This book is about grief, pain, loss, faith, and new beginnings. I hope that you can tell from my scribbles that I know the subjects very well. I also hope that if you are reading this in an effort to help you through a tough time that I have helped in some small way.

In some ways, this book has been very difficult. As I said, I have a history of false starts and unfinished works. I have had to work at being disciplined enough to put some words into the laptop on a daily basis. There are always excuses; I'm sick, busy at work, tired, traveling, etc. There are times when I sit down to type and nothing comes to mind.

In other ways, this project has been very easy. I can be driving, sitting in church, watching TV and a line or two will pop into my head. I jot it down so it is not lost and then get to my computer as soon as I can. What starts as a line or two easily flows into a poem.

One of my favorite writers is Stephen King. I've had my picture taken in front of his house in Bangor, Maine. He often writes about the writing process. He has said many times that the stories pop into his head and he just writes them down. During this project, I've come to understand what he means.

April 12, 2015
I recently watched a YouTube clip of Bob Hope and James Cagney doing a soft-shoe routine. For those of you too young to know what I'm talking about, look it up on YouTube.

Watching the clip, I was struck with a couple of thoughts. First, neither of these two stars was famous for their dancing skills. Hope was a comedian and Cagney made a name playing gangsters on film. The dance routine showed two very skilled tap dancers, Cagney, IMHO being slightly more talented. I smiled throughout the routine. Cagney has been gone for about 30 years and Hope about 15, yet here they are still making me smile. Marie has been gone five months and the wound is still raw.

I have no video or voice recordings of her. I do have photographs and memories. In the first few months, a picture or a memory would instantly bring tears. I'm not done with the tears yet however, now there are smiles mixed with them. I hope, in time, that family, friends, and I will be able to share memories and smile and laugh. Just like Cagney and Hope, Marie will live in our hearts and thinking of her will bring joy.

April 13, 2015
Smile
Why not smile? Life is too short
to walk with a frown for even a mile.
Be a friend. We all need someone
who will be there in the end.
Walk with me. Don't be in a hurry
there is so much for us to see.
Hold my hand, There's no need to walk alone
while we are exploring this magical land.
Help a stranger. You were given gifts to share
and you never know when you'll be the one in danger.
Be a grown up. Don't play middle school games. That's not what
you profess when you drink from the cup.
Follow the rules. Otherwise you might end up
in a place full of fools.

Remember to listen. There is a world of stories
some will make your eyes glisten.
Eat some cake. Kale and carrots are fine
but someone loving took time to bake.
Dream a dream. Working to pay bills will get old
get people who dare on your team.
Do not shove. Your turn will come
Just live, laugh, and love.

April 14, 2015
It Takes a Village
The last few months have been quite a learning experience for me.
While I am no expert on grief, I have learned a lot about it and
myself. Here are some thoughts on the subject.

Grief is both individual and communal. It is individual in that
each of us finds our own way of grieving and coping with the
pain. Some wallow in sorrow. Some deny the pain. Others seek
counseling. I write. There is no right or wrong way to do it. You
have to find what works for you.

Grief is also communal. I lost my wife. My children lost their
mother. To others, Marie was a sister, niece, cousin, treasured
friend. We are all dealing with loss, trying to find our way to a new
normal.

Throughout this process, I have received amazing support from
family, friends, and my church. I will forever be grateful for this
support. As you know, writing has been my way of expressing,
confronting, and dealing with my grief. I have received many
positive comments both on Facebook and in person. Some of my
posts have brought smiles of fond remembrance while others
have caused tears.

Please know that if reading them brought tears, writing them did
as well. The tears have been cleansing and slowly sad tears are
turning to tears of joy. As time goes by, pain is replaced with
happy memories. Life does go on. Live, laugh, love.

April 15, 2015
Wings
Every time a bell rings
an angel gets her wings
when a good deed is done

and you've helped someone
you'll probably get a hug
and get bitten by the heart bug
Try not to be greedy
too many are needy
you have so much to share
so show people you care
The best way to live
is always to give
Care more about others
we're all sisters and brothers
When life gets you down
don't waste time with a frown
Show someone your smile
and laugh every once in a while
Love with all your heart
you never know when you'll part
I will always remember
Marie got her wings last November.

April 16, 2015
Live
If you have been following my posts, you have seen my sign off:
live, laugh, love. They are words I live by and encourage others to
do the same. Why do I promote this?

It started when Marie was in the hospital. Each room has a
whiteboard and markers. It is used for staff communication. On it
you find names of the duty nurse, aide, and other information.
There is also a space marked "Goals."

Usually, underneath it will say, "walk ten steps," "breathe without
oxygen," or other physical therapy goals. On one visit, the space
was empty. To encourage Marie, I wrote, "Today's goals are: Live,
Laugh, and Love."

Obviously, the first goal for everyone should be to live. In her
case, that meant survive. For us, it should mean thrive, live life to
the fullest. Explore, experience, challenge yourself. "Laugh"
comes from the story of a cancer patient who cured himself by
watching old movies and comedy routines that made him laugh
heartily on a daily basis. I figured it worked once, why not try
again? Besides, I love to laugh.

The last, "Love," is the most important. Life without love is not life. Love your neighbor, love your family, love your friends, love your God, and, yes, love yourself.

Life, lived fully, is great. Laughter makes it more fun. Love makes it worth living. After Marie's death, I went to look for a picture frame. In the store, I saw a picture with the following phrase: Live well, Laugh often, and Love with all your heart. That picture now hangs on my wall. Live, laugh, love.

April 17, 2015
Trust
I sometimes feel like a man on a wire
walking between joy and pain
Always looking higher
trying to stay sane
I lost my wife
she flew off like a dove
while she was my life
I have found a new love
And now, day after day
I laugh and I cry
nothing more to say
you know I never lie
God moves me where he wants me
I trust he has a plan
the path is sometimes hard to see
but I follow the best I can
though I have lost something great
her loss too great to measure
there's a new woman I date
who really is a treasure
friends and family try to adjust
they're meeting someone new
I only ask for their trust
it's really all I can do.

April 18, 2015
Written in a sidewalk at Penn State is the saying, "Each of us is ultimately alone." I read this many times, walking to and from my classes. That is a very heavy concept for a 17-year-old to wrap his head around. It was also, I realize now, a part of my maturation process.

I grew up with two parents and four siblings. I was rarely, if ever, alone. As a freshman on a large campus, I was frequently alone. I was trying to find my way, figure out where I fit, and who I was. I was no longer my parents' son or one of the McClellan boys. I was Dave. I was alone.

I learned that that was okay. It gave me time to think. It gave me a chance to figure out that I was capable of facing the world on my own. Marie and I married shortly after college. Then along came our two kids. Between work and family, once again, I was rarely alone. Kristy and Brad grew up and flew the coop. When Marie left us, I was alone. This was a different kind of alone. This was a painful, lonely alone.

Friends and family tried to comfort me. Their efforts made me feel even more alone. I could see in their eyes that they were seeing me as somehow different. Instead of being part of a team, I was flying solo. They didn't know and I didn't know how, or if, I fit into the group. So, even when I was with a group of friends, I felt lonely. The time I spent alone, took me back to when I was 17. Once again, I had to figure out who I was and how I fit in.

This time, I had my faith and a closer relationship with God. I found I needed to be alone and quiet to hear Him. When I was alone and quiet, He said over and over, "You are going to be okay. I will take care of you. Your work is not done."

Over time, though still alone, I was no longer lonely. I started becoming more comfortable with who I was. I knew that I did not want to spend the rest of my life alone. I also knew I would not find a new partner if I was in a corner crying or spending all my time with my old circle of friends. I had to get out of the house and meet new people. I also had to be, at times, alone. I had to be quiet. I had to listen to God.

April 19, 2015
I was going through papers in my desk today when I came across a folded sheet of paper. I unfolded it and found the logo for the company where Marie worked for many years. It was a copy of an email sent to her by the owner of the company. It was sent just six months before her diagnosis. I read it through my tears.

As I approach my twilight years, I am struck by the inevitability that the party must end. And one clear, cold morning after I'm gone, my spouse will awaken in the warmth of our bedroom and be struck with the pain of learning that sometimes there isn't any "more."

No more hugs, no more special moments to celebrate together, no more phone calls just to chat, no more "just one minute." Sometimes what we care about the most gets all used up and goes away, never to return before we can say good-bye, say "I love you."

So while we have it, it's best we love it, care for it, fix it when it's broken, and heal it when it's sick. This is true for marriage…and old cars. And children with bad report cards, dogs, with bad hips, and aging parents and grandparents. We keep them because they are worth it, because we are worth it. Some things we keep, like a best friend who moved away, or a sister-in-law after a divorce. There are just some things that make us happy no matter what.

Let every one of your friends know your true feelings, even if you think they don't love you back.

April 20, 2015
Angels
To provide a break from the stress of annual testing, the students at Broughal Middle School were treated to a performance at Zoellner Art Center. I was very proud of all the students as they were well behaved and respectful during the performance.

The show was a combination of ballet and modern dance. While I am not a fan of the art form, I admit I found the first act hauntingly beautiful. It began with a young man and a young lady in an embrace, illuminated by dozens of pinpoint spots. They began a dance with the young lovers coming together, drifting apart, and coming together again. As the young man exits the stage, she is lifted skyward. As she is lowered to the stage, she is surrounded by four dancers clad in white. As they dance around her, she also dons a white dress. I interpreted it to mean she became an angel. Fortunately, the theater was dark and no students saw me crying.

April 21, 2015
Judges
To whom shall my love go
It's not based on an algorithm , you know

In love again I will fall
Will she be short or will she be tall
Will it be a year, a month, or a few days
Who makes the rules, who says
Did you plan who would make your heart leap
Did a computer tell you whose company to keep
I don't know why
Marie had to die
She left way too soon
Leaving me crying like a loon
Before she left, she said Don't be alone
Find someone new to call your own
I did not know I would find
Someone so warm and kind
As quickly as I did
Should I have hid
Should I apologize
For looking in her eyes
I am going to live my life
I will go on without my wife
I want this woman by my side
Or on my scooter when I ride
I want to know who
Will judge me, You, You, You?
I will give you a task

Be happy for me, it's all I ask.

During Marie's ordeal, both of our children put their lives on hold and came to spend time with their mom and help with her care. Near the end, my daughter informed me that she would not do it again. If I got sick, I would be on my own. Her mother's death hurt her deeply and affected her to the point that getting through each day was difficult. I had a similar reaction to my father's death. This is just one more reason that I prefer the idea of a heart attack over cancer.

April 22, 2015
Faith is what has gotten me through
Those tough times when I was feeling blue
When she left me all alone
I could not cope on my own
I needed someone by my side
To know that He was along for the ride
I could not have gotten through days of pain
When my tears were falling like rain

If I did not know that He was there
That I was always in His care
He sheltered me in his arm
And kept me from further harm
He whispered in my ear
Do not shed another tear
Trust me when I say
I will get you through this day
Your work on Earth is not done
You have things to do, my son
So get up, get going
There is no time for slowing
It is time to move
To find a new groove
You can't live in the past
The only thing that will last
You will find that it's true
Is my enduring Love for you.

April 23, 2015
If there was a way to talk to someone in Heaven, who would you call? What questions would you ask? What would you want to tell them? Was there something left unsaid before they left?

Let's turn it around. Is there someone still here that you love? Have you told them TODAY that you love them? Is there something unsaid that you want them to know? Hold her hand, give her flowers, tell her you love her, now, while you still can.

April 24, 2015
In the early morning hours
My tears fall like showers
I have to face another day
Knowing she has gone away
Put one foot in front of the other
Knowing my kids have lost their mother
Minutes seem to drag
My spirits flag
In the middle of the day
I feel a Sun's ray
Warming my shoulder
Making me a little bolder
Though death has taken its toll
I feel I'm climbing out of my hole

Marie is watching over me
Telling me to live and be free
Then in the quiet evening
I hear a gentle voice sing
We had our time together
Now it's time to cut the tether
You have to move on
Now that I'm gone
And find a way to be
Who you are without me

April 25, 2015
We go through life and collect things
Clothes and cars and rings
We go to the store and buy, buy, buy
Sometimes we don't even know why
Maybe we got a sad letter
Buying something will make us feel better
We surround ourselves
With Santas and elves
We fill our pantry
With flour and candy
And the bigger boys
Get more expensive toys
It's only when life shatters
We figure out what matters
The people around us
The Love that has found us
The people who are dear
We want to hold near
Enough is enough
Get rid of the stuff
Put a smile on your mug
And give someone a hug
Find someone you'll miss
And give them a kiss
Don't wait
Go out on a date
Before this day is through
Say to someone, I love you

April 26, 2015
Every day a teardrop brings me closer to finding my way in a
world without her.

Little Things
It's the little things
you never know what the day brings
sometimes tears fall like rain
your heart all full of pain
you really miss her
you want to kiss her
one more time
all you can do is rhyme
trying to let your feelings out
you don't want to sit and pout
you want to celebrate
a very important date
what was really hard
was the birthday card
the last we had
that was signed, "Love, Mom and Dad."

I was going through a stack of papers when I found a birthday card that Marie had purchased for our son. She always prepared months in advance for Christmas and birthdays. She signed the card, "Love, Mom and Dad." I gave it to Brad for his 26th birthday.

April 28, 2015
Yes, I am going away
You are going to stay
Even though I am still young
My work here is done
You have to keep a brave face
And know I'm in a better place
I don't know how long
You'll have to stay strong
For our two children
For a time will come when
They will be very sad
And really need their Dad
And for our friends
Who stay when my life ends
You have to live
And learn to forgive
So be strong
And carry on

And when you feel pain
Know that I remain
Just like at the start
Always in your heart

April 29, 2015
Away
She's gone
Where is she
Why did she leave
What am I to do
We did not plan for this
I did not know she would die young
We did not plan for this
What am I to do
Why did she leave
Where is she
She's gone
Away

April 30, 2015
Slow
Take it slow
be careful where you go
there are no maps
nor any phone apps
telling you how to proceed
what you really need
is friends you can trust
and family who will just
Love you no matter which way
you decide to go today
you have to be smart
and listen to your heart
you can't change the past
Her memories will last
and you are still here
your final day is not near
with so many days left to live
and so much more to give
just do the right things
and see what tomorrow brings

<u>May 1, 2015</u>
Thief
Death comes like a thief
and steals the one you love
leaves you mired in grief
questioning the One above
you go on with your living
doing the best you can
trying to be forgiving
of your fellow man
It's not their fault she died
it does no good to cry
some of her doctors lied
when they really did try
to kill the beast within
they said we'll try the latest
recently approved medicine
though it was the greatest
she really had no chance
there's no use trying to fight
when the Devil wants to dance
and it's your time to see the Light
she has gone to her glory
and I miss her so
there is more to my story
many miles left to go
that is why at night
as many of you know
when I hurt, I write.

<u>May 2, 2015</u>
Picking up the pieces
Of a life that was shattered
One is gone
One left to carry on
In my house
I walk alone
Wiping tears that will not stop
In a crowd
I walk alone
With no hand to hold
In my church
I sit alone
Feeling cold where once was warmth

In my school
Though not alone
I wipe children's tears
While holding back my own
In my life
I am alone
I once said
Til death do us part
I did not know
I would take it to heart
Without my wife
I am alone
Making my way
In a strange new world
Picking up the pieces
Of a life that was shattered

May 3, 2015
I woke up today and saw the sun peeking through the clouds.
Dark and gray with a threat of rain, but still the day holds
promise. The sun will battle the clouds for control of the sky. Will
the clouds shrivel and die? Or, will they gather their friends and
cover the sky?

It may rain today, tomorrow, and the next. People will hide
indoors or sulk under umbrellas. When will this end? It can't rain
forever, can it? One day, I guarantee, the sun will win and come
out again. People will come out, look up, and smile.

May 4, 2015
Friends
I know I'm not the only one to cry
others also have lost
and are still paying the cost
still I wonder why
friends can't be happy for me
why they cannot see
how important it is they try
to get to know Cyn
to find a place to begin
I am not going to lie
it hurts when they turn their back
when common courtesy they lack
If you hear me sigh

117

it's because in the end
I lost my wife and now I need you, friend

May 5, 2015
How long will you live
What answer will you give
Long enough to write a book
Travel the world and have a look
To save a life
To take a wife
To really go wild
Or calm down and have a child
Will you sit around wishing
Or take some time to go fishing
Will you make new friends
Or go where the map ends
To climb up a mountain
Or tour the Trevi Fountain
Will you sit there and stew
Or invent something new
Do you know how long
Til you finish your song
It comes down to this
The point you cannot miss
Since no one knows the date
You've got things to do, don't wait

May 6, 2015
Brad
Due in June, he showed up in May
The Doc said, "C-section, okay?"
Our new little mister
Came to join his big sister
A girl we had one, a boy we had one
There are no other choices, so we were done
The case was open and shut
He was our little Peanut
Though not very large
He thought he was in charge
Baseball, football
He tried them all
But didn't get a locker
Until he tried soccer
It got expensive when he chose

To punch a bully in the nose
But as the case unfolded
The assistant principal got scolded
And so Brad
Just like his Dad
Succumbed to fate
And enrolled at Penn State
In college he was plotting
A career in mascotting
I said to my boy
Find something you enjoy
He said listen right here
I really like beer
Though his story is far from ending
Right now he is bartending
I know someday
He'll find his way
He just needs a little elf
To tell him to believe in himself
Happy birthday, Brad!

May 7, 2015
Trust
They pulled down the curtain
now my future's uncertain
will I get a class and teach
or retire and head for a beach
who knows where will I reside
in the great white north or ocean side
will I be in a middle school
or will elementary students find me cool
will I be sweeping floors
or welcoming kids in through my doors
are the students going to be tall
or really quite small
will we pass in the hall
or say hi in the mall
my plans are grand
in front of a class I will stand
and young minds I will reach
as each new day I will teach
of this I am sure
as I watch them mature
I'm one of the rare few

who really loves what I do
I put my trust in the One
that I'll do this before I am done.

In the midst of dealing with my grief, I was also searching for my first teaching job. After working in lumber yards for many years, I returned to college and got my Masters degree and a teaching certificate. Teaching jobs are hard to come by in Pennsylvania. This was written after another unsuccessful interview.

<u>May 8, 2015</u>
You live in a nice house. You drive a decent car. You have a job that pays the bills. You have a wife and a family. Then the clouds roll in. Someone sets your house on fire. No big deal, you have insurance. So you live in a motel while they fix your house. Life goes on.

You have a car accident. You have insurance. You get a rental while they fix your car. No big deal. Life goes on.

Your wife gets cancer and passes away. ...... Sure, you have insurance so the bills still get paid. Sure, your life goes on.

However, it is a big deal. Nothing will ever be the same. Going on after losing a spouse is kind of like being a stroke victim. A person that suffers a stroke and survives has to re-learn basic skills; how to tie shoes, button shirts, hold a spoon, how to speak. When you lose your spouse, you have to learn how to balance a checkbook, pay bills, iron shirts, do laundry.....how to fall asleep in a bed by yourself. Life does go on, but the world is a very different place.

<u>May 9, 2015</u>
I Googled "advice for a surviving spouse." Seven of the first eight recommended sites dealt with finances.

Finances are important, and are definitely a source of concern when you lose a partner. That being said, that wasn't the advice I was seeking. One site did have the type of advice I had in mind -- expertbeacon.com/advice-surviving-death-spouse-or-partner-young-age/.

Though the tips are aimed at younger people, I feel the advice works for any age. The site included a list of do's and don'ts:

"Do
- talk about your loss
- find a support system
- practice self-care
- grieve at your own pace
- honor your loved one's memory

Don't
- isolate yourself
- try to "get over" it
- deny your grief
- expect others to know what you need
- be too hard on yourself"

I think I did the do's and avoided most of the don'ts. I talked about losing Marie with friends, family, and clergy. I also, obviously, shared my feelings on Facebook and now in this book. All of that has been tremendously therapeutic.

As I mentioned, my support system consisted of family, friends, and clergy. I practiced self-care by cooking healthy meals even when I was not hungry or in the mood to eat. I am grieving at my own pace, even though some would say I moved on too quickly.

Yes, I am in a new relationship. That does not mean I am no longer grieving. I learned you can't hide from the tears by staying busy. When it hits, stop, cry, experience it. I am honoring Marie's memory by writing this book. She always cared about others more than herself. If this book can help someone who is grieving, then Marie, in a way, helped them.

Don't isolate yourself. I made regular runs to the grocery store, bank, and church. I also got out to sing karaoke once a week. There were times I was not in a fun mood and would rather have stayed home. I knew that could become a habit and didn't want to live like that. Don't deny your grief. If someone says, "How are you?", tell them, "I'm hurting and could use a hug." People want to help.

Don't expect others to know what you need? That is a tough one. There are many times when I don't know what I need. I will say this, don't be angry at happy people around you. Instead of letting your grief bring them down, allow their joy to pick you up.

Don't be too hard on yourself. What if I had been a better husband, what if we had gone to a different doctor, I should have done this, I shouldn't have done that… none of that thinking changes or improves the situation. If you made mistakes, learn from them and try to be a better person if you get a second chance.

The last sentence on the site is one of hope, which concisely says what I am taking a book to say: "It is possible to move forward and live a whole-hearted and fulfilling life once again. It will just take time, and it is okay to move at your own pace.

May 10, 2015
As the world sleeps
A man lays awake and weeps
For many hours
He thinks about the flowers
He should have bought for her
The world wakes up
And he drinks a cup
Then he writes a line
Of poetry so fine
He should have written it for her
The world goes on its way
Just another day
He goes for a walk
Just around the block
He should have walked with her
The world sits down to eat
No one left in the street
He puts on his hat
Just wanting to chat
He should have talked with her
The world goes to bed
Thoughts race in his head
He just wishes he had known
How soon she would be gone
He should have said, "I love you" to her

May 11, 2015
Two
Lives shared
forever paired
you'll have time to laugh

your sorrows cut in half
no more trouble
your joys will double
when find your match
your dreams will hatch
it's better to be two
than to be just you
oh, the places you'll see
how much fun it will be
it's easy to be brave
when you have someone to save
and if you have a care
you know she'll be there
there's no need to hurry
you don't have to worry
it is as it seems
she's the girl of your dreams

My new relationship was flourishing at this point, and I was again experiencing joy in my life.

<u>May 12, 2015</u>
Morning Dew
I am not done crying
yet I am still trying
to go on with my life
without my darling wife
her recent departing
is definitely still smarting
I cry for what I lost
never knowing the cost
she meant so much
her loss was such
that I start anew
my tears like morning dew
always near
waiting to appear
good times or bad
I didn't know what I had
I've learned a lot
and if I get another shot
at Love, I know it
that every day I will show it

<u>May 13, 2015</u>
I am awake. This day is another gift from God. We were going to grow old together, retire, travel.

God had other plans. He ended her struggle, her pain. He took her home. I know He has a plan for me as well. I am left to carry on, to chart a new path. Where will it lead?

I read a book by Billie Letts called The Honk and Holler Opening Soon. One character is a Vietnamese man living in America. He is waiting for his wife to join him. To do so, she must take a boat. His friend asked him where the boat would go after leaving Viet Nam. His response talks about fate:

"She leave Vietnam in boat, then boat go where boat go."
"What does that mean?"
"Sometime boat go to Thailand, sometime Malaysia, sometime Indonesia. Boat go where boat go." He shrugged then to show he understood the nature of fate.

Boat go where boat go. It can take years to understand that. You can also look at Jonah. God had a plan. He wanted Jonah to go to Ninevah. Jonah did not want to go. A great fish took him to Ninevah.

Yes, we have free will. Yes, we make choices. I sincerely believe that everything happens for a reason. Every choice we make leads to the same result. When all is said and done, we end up where we are meant to be. Boat go where boat go.

<u>May 14, 2015</u>
No man is an island. We have all heard that saying. We humans are social animals. We are not meant to live in isolation. That is something to remember when we are grieving.

When you lose a spouse, it can be very tempting to crawl into a hole and cry. Don't do it. Find reasons to get out and interact with people. I made regular trips to the grocery store. It helped in several ways. It got me out of the house. I got to do something to get my mind out of grieving mode. I got to talk to the cashiers. And, I got to eat fresh, healthy meals.

I also attended church. That was a double-edged sword. It got me out of the house and helped me keep my relationship with God strong. On the other hand, everyone at church knew Marie. Whenever I attended, some people would try to console and some would pretend I wasn't there as they didn't know what to say. A precious few simply treated me like a friend.

When Cynthia started attending with me, I knew it was time to look for a new church. Most of my former friends made no attempt to get to know her, and some were openly hostile. Although I (as my religion teaches) forgive them, I would not continue to subject Cynthia to their rude behavior. I resigned my seat on Consistory and asked to be removed from the membership roll. Wherever we end up, we will do some church shopping.

May 15, 2015
Calendar
I am walking through a jungle. I am in uncharted territory. I know where I want to go; however, I'm not sure which path to take. On some days, there is a path and travel is easy. Other days, the path disappears and I am forced to hack my way through dense undergrowth. There are some days which are even more difficult. One misstep and I spend the day slogging through quicksand. Minutes seem like hours.

Though there are many sunny, happy days, there are still days filled with rain and pain. One would think a calendar would have no effect or control in our lives. One day is like the next. The earth spins on its axis, the sun rises and sets, the moon winks hello and goodbye.

I've learned that is not the case. There are days on the calendar that are set with snares, ready to overwhelm you with memories and force you to relive the pain and heartache. February 6: her birthday. One Sunday in May: Mothers Day. September 30: our anniversary. A Thursday in November: Thanksgiving. December 1: my birthday. December. 25: Christmas. And, to end the year, December 31, the night we met.

I am told that as time passes, pain eases and tears fall less often. For now, with the help of friends, family, and my new love, I will continue to hack through the jungle. I will live, laugh, and love. I will reach my destination.

As part of my grieving process, I wrote poetry (obviously). I also read poetry about grieving. Here is a sample. The author is unknown but he clearly knows my heart.

YOU NEVER SAID GOODBYE
Author Unknown

You never said I'm leaving
You never said goodbye.
You were gone before I knew it,
And only God knew why.
A million times I needed you,
A million times I cried.
If love alone could have saved you,
You never would have died.
In life I loved you dearly,
In death I love you still.
In my heart you hold a place,
That no one could ever fill.
It broke my heart to lose you,
But you didn't go alone
For part of me went with you,
The day God took you home.

May 17, 2015
Kristy
She is my treasure
Her worth beyond measure
Before she was born, it was me and my wife
She came along and changed my life
Every father wants a son
But when all is said and done
If she had been a boy
She would not have brought such joy
As a baby, she would cry for a while
Then tears were replaced by a beautiful smile
She made friends with ease
Always eager to please
Though usually mellow
She never liked Jello
Just like her mom
She twirled baton

She was no one's fool
And breezed through school
Never had a fight
Even learned to spell bright
It was something called fate
That she followed her dad to Dear Old State
Where she learned how to drink
And bumped her chin on a sink
Such a good student
Her society made her president
Then Lucas came along
With a Dave Matthews song
And they decided to be
A couple, you see
After a stop in New Jersey
They moved way up north by the sea
If they are not hiking
They are probably biking
What they think is just as nice
Is climbing up some ice
And after visiting out West
They decided Calgary was best
Though now we're miles away
I think of her every day
And my eyes get misty
When I think of my dear Kristy
Happy birthday, Kristy!

May 18, 2015
Everyone, if they live long enough, experiences the death of a loved one. Most of us never share our feelings outside of a close circle of family and friends.

Celebrities, like us, also experience loss. Unlike us, they have a wider audience when they share their feelings. Liam Neeson lost his beautiful wife, Natasha Richardson to a skiing accident. Several years later, he shared his thoughts:

"It hits you. It's like a wave. You just get this profound feeling of instability...the Earth isn't stable anymore and then it passes and it becomes more infrequent, but I still get it sometimes," he said. "There's periods now in our New York residence when I hear the door opening, especially the first couple of years… anytime I hear that door opening, I still think I'm going to hear her."

"They say the hardest thing in the world is losing someone you love. Someone you grew old with and watched grow everyday. Someone who showed you how to love. It's the worst thing to ever happen to anyone. My wife died unexpectedly. She brought me so much joy. She was my everything. Those 16 years of being her husband taught me how to love unconditionally.

We have to stop and be thankful for our spouses. Because, life is very short. Spend time with your spouses. Treat them well. Because, one day, when you look up from your phone, they won't be there anymore. What I truly learned most of all is, live and love everyday like it's your last. Because one day, it will be. Take chances and go live life. Tell the ones you love, that you love them everyday. Don't take any moment for granted. Life is worth living."
Liam Neeson is a well known, respected actor. I worked in lumber yards and am now a teacher. Though our lives are drastically different, we do share common feelings on losing your spouse.

May 19, 2015
Tell me why
Men don't cry
Tell me again
They don't feel pain?
When someone dies
Do they close their eyes
And play pretend
That life didn't end
Just say, "So long."
Hey, life goes on
Or do they stumble a little
when they walk
Does their voice crack a little
when they talk
Has their heart
Been torn apart
Do they feel a tug
To ask for a hug
Do they wish they were bolder
Do they long for a shoulder
On which they could cry

May 20, 2015
You know those kiddie rides at carnivals? The rides are miniature roller coasters. They have cars with steering wheels. The kids ride along, turning the steering wheel left and right. The car pays no attention; it follows the track. You can call it fate, destiny, or the Master Plan.

Call it what you like, I believe that life is like that ride. You move along in life, making decisions. You think you are calling the shots. Then, somehow, years later, you wind up somewhere you never planned on being. I have found it easier to take my hands off the wheel and enjoy the ride. My most common prayer is, "Your will be done, Lord."

May 21, 2015
Contemplation
I lost my wife a little over six months ago. As a way for me to deal with my grief, I began writing about my feelings and posting them. At first, it was cathartic and I received much support from my Facebook friends. When Marie was diagnosed, she told me to find someone new. She and God agreed that I should not be alone.

In January, a beautiful and caring woman entered life. My usually morose posts took a decided turn back to bright happiness. Since then, the amount of people who "like" my posts has dropped significantly and some friends have been less than welcoming to my newfound love. If you watch the evening news, you normally see twenty nine minutes of death and destruction and one minute of warm, fuzzy, good news. I guess people prefer bad news over good. Perhaps other people's suffering makes them feel better about their own circumstances. Whatever, I forgive them. I, no, we will go on. We will live, laugh, and love. I pray that some of you will join us in our happiness.

With a few exceptions, many of my friends and family have turned their backs on me. When most of them first met Cynthia, she was still reeling from her divorce and her mother's death. They did not get to see the loving, caring woman that I know her to be. I only wish they would open their hearts to her.

May 22, 2015
Til death do us part
Words straight from the heart
In for a kiss he leans
Does he know what it means?
It doesn't mean forever
That she'll leave you never
There will come a day
One will go away
When you think you are winning
You'll need a new beginning
Though your friends still care
You're no longer a pair
You have to find a new road
While carrying a heavy load
Make a new trail
Find new rivers to sail
One day take a chance
And explore a new romance
Though your heart still aches
You have what it takes
To do what you have to do
And begin anew

May 23, 2015
Crossroads
I'm at the crossroads
where happy meets sad
carrying the loads
of both good and bad
I smile through tears
remembering the years
that we shared
and the friends who cared
Sweet Caroline was her favorite song
and it makes me long
for days long ago
when I loved her so
Now, a new girl is here
to dry my tear
she makes me laugh
my new better half

when she is near
I have no fear
I face the future knowing
our love will keep growing
though tears will still flow
smiles are sure to follow

May 24, 2015
Five o'clock in the morning
The only one up is me
I was given no warning
That this is how it would be
Everything was going well
Until the doctor said
Your life is going to Hell
Marie is going to die in bed
You'll have to make some changes
Get used to being on your own
As your schedule rearranges
To fit a life lived alone
No more dinners for two
No more hand to hold
You'll sit alone in the pew
As the church bulletin you unfold
You'll go alone to the grocery store
And shop for meals for one
The times you shop for four
Are gone and done
It's just not fair
Why did you take
The girl with golden hair
A new life I have to make
I just need a little faith

May 25, 2015
I am a rock. I am an island. And a rock feels no pain, and an island never cries.

May 26, 2015
"I know how you feel. My dog died last year."
"I know how you feel, my mom died two years ago."
Etc.

Thank you for commiserating with me. With all due respect, you have NO FUCKING IDEA how I feel. I have lost several dogs. Losing the last one ripped my heart out. I lost my dad several years ago and it messed me up for two years. Neither of those losses compare to losing your spouse. Everything in your life changes. Everything. I have learned quite a lot about life going through this grieving process. One thing I learned is to never say, "I know how you feel." You can say, "I feel bad for you, I miss her too." Just don't say, "I know how you feel."

May 27, 2015
I found this poem online, author unknown. I found it comforting.

As I sit in heaven
And watch you everyday
I try to let you know with signs
I never went away
I hear you when you're laughing
And watch you as you sleep
I even place my arms around you
To calm you as you weep
I see you wish the days away
Begging to have me home
So I try to send you signs
So you know you are not alone
Don't feel guilty that you have
Life that was denied to me
Heaven is truly beautiful
Just you wait and see
So live your life, laugh again
Enjoy yourself, be free
Then I know with every breath you take
You'll be taking one for me

May 28, 2015
After a sad and dark holiday weekend, some sunlight returned to my life. Hopefully, there will be more to follow as things develop.

My holidays had always been spent with friends and relatives. But I received no invitations to any of the parties that were held this Memorial Day weekend. Like the old song, "You and Me Against the World," sometimes it seems like it's Cyn and me against the world. That's okay, because Cyn and I make a pretty good team.

<u>May 29, 2015</u>
The beautiful girl with bright blue eyes
Now watches over me from the skies
Years ago, we said, "I do."
Not knowing ours years together would be so few
Our life together had just begun
No one plans on dying young
Our true future was unseen
Lulled to complacency by routine
Working hard to pay our bills
Never bothered with any ills
We were going to retire
Travel to our hearts desire
Our new address would be the road
Our motorhome carrying the load
Our plans were not meant to be
God decided to take her from me
All of our plans have been burned
And a few new lessons I have learned
No life is free of sorrow
And no one is guaranteed tomorrow
Make the most of each day
Say the things you long to say
Live your life without regret
Laugh every chance you get
Love with all your heart
In case your lover has to part

<u>May 30, 2015</u>
If I had a chance to talk to God
I would have just one question:
Why?
Why is there cancer?
Why is there hunger?
Why is there hate?
Why is there murder?
Why can't we get along?
I know what He would say
There is no cancer in Heaven
There is no hunger in Heaven
There is no hate in Heaven
There is no murder in Heaven
Everyone gets along in Heaven
You see, I love you so very much

I want you to be with me in Heaven
So I sent my Son to live with you
He saw cancer
He saw hunger
He was hated
He was murdered
People could not get along with Him
He opened the door to Heaven
And offered an end to cancer
Offered an end to hunger
Offered an end to hate
Offered an end to murder
Offered a chance to get along

May 31, 2015
I am not used to living alone. There are days when there is no one
to talk to except Lady, my collie. She's not much at conversation.

"Ruff!, I have to go out."
"Ruff!, I'm hungry."
"Ruff! -- Nothing really, I just wanted to bark!"

I find myself talking to her anyway. At least I'm not talking to
myself; that would be crazy. Lady is a good listener and is always
willing to offer a shoulder to cry on. Thank you, God, for giving
us dogs.

Marie and I both loved dogs. We went through the cycle of getting a
dog, loving the dog, and losing the dog. Each time, Marie would say,
"Never again. It hurts too much when they die."

I am not meant to be alone and I am not meant to be without a dog.
After losing a dog, I would lobby for a new one. I would find a picture of
a puppy and show it to Marie.

"Isn't it cute?"

She could only resist for so long. Though we loved all of our dogs,
Simba was special. He was a German Shepherd/Border Collie mix.
Imagine a Shepherd with floppy ears. He was a lovable dog, but if
someone came into our house and didn't pet him, look out. He would put
his ears down and growl. He would stop when I scolded him. He was also
very smart. He would come in and wake me in the morning to take me for
his morning constitutional.

One morning, he came in and did his little dance. I got up and put
shoes on only to find he had taken my place in the bed. He had been

setting me up that whole time. I couldn't be mad at him; he outsmarted me.

When we lost him to cancer, Marie said, "Never again. No more dogs." It took a year of relentless campaigning on my part before she gave in. She showed me a picture of a tri-color collie and said, "Find this dog and we can get a dog."

It took about five minutes on the internet to find an Amish Collie breeder in Lancaster that had puppies. It just happened that we had a camping trip scheduled that would put us in Lancaster. Our friends went with us to help us choose a puppy. The tri-color that we wanted was limping. Not wanting to take a chance, we picked a little girl who looks just like Lassie and named her Lady Daisy May.

We were all excited about the new puppy, except for my friend. We asked why he seemed sad. He said, "I never had a puppy."

He was 50 years old and had never experienced having a puppy! When we got back to the campground, Marie said I should go online and find another puppy. She was going to buy our friend a puppy. After a little research, we found one about an hour away. We made up some pretext to take a road trip with our friends. When we arrived at the farm, we told our friend to pick a puppy, our treat.

He picked a puppy that could have been Lady's twin and named her RoseMarie. Rosie and Lady were born 11 days apart and spent many happy hours playing together.

Lady was three when Marie left us. I don't know how I would have done without her there to comfort me on those long, lonely nights that followed. Though I always wanted to have two dogs, Marie did not. We always had one or none.

Cynthia and I bought a Mini-Chorkie that we named Nittany. She is a mix of Chihuahua and Yorkie and will never weigh more than five pounds -- a purse dog.

She is fun to have around and it is comical to watch her bully the much larger Lady. Lady likes to play fetch. Before Nittany, I would throw a toy, Lady would chase it and bring it back. We would do this until she got bored and went back to sleep. Now, I throw a toy, Nittany grabs it and puts it in a pile of "her stuff." If Lady happens to get to the toy first, Nittany takes it out of her mouth and adds it to her pile. If Lady and I want to play, I put bossy in her crate.

June 1, 2015
I am not the man I used to be
I had a wife aside of me
I'm sad to say

She went away
Leaving me to grieve
I have to start a new life
Without my loving wife
Cancer took her from me
Death set her free
Leaving me to grieve
Where once stood many a friend
That's all come to an end
They chose to ignore
The new girl I adore
Leaving me to grieve
My daughter Kristy and son Brad
Are shunning dear old dad
Because I want to begin
A new life with Cyn
Leaving me to grieve
If you know someone
Whose spouse is now gone
Do not make them plead
Be a friend indeed
Don't leave them alone to grieve

PART FIVE: SUMMER AGAIN

June 2, 2015
Friends
When I began this journey
several years ago
there was a lady by my side
now I'm walking in a shadow
ever since the lady died
Friends used to gather round us
when the lady was my wife
now they are gone
since she lost her life
they've left me one by one
someone new has joined me in my travels
a beautiful, caring lady
has brought back some light
the shadows aren't so shady
the path once again bright
I will one day reach my destination
I hope friends gather near
to me and my new love
that they will lose their fear
with a little help from above.

Ahh…rain! There is nothing like it. It is summertime. It is hot and muggy. It is silent outside because people are hiding in their air conditioned houses and animals are sleeping in the shade. Any discussions begin with, "Man, it is hot!"

You can smell the heat in the tarry smell of hot asphalt, the dead bird baking in the street, and the aroma of garbage cooking in the can. Boom! Zzzap! A late afternoon thunderstorm brings some relief. It pours.

Though it doesn't last long, the changes it brings are amazing. The temperature and humidity have both dropped. The nasty smells have been replaced by sweet and fresh. People come out to drink it in. Birds start chirping, dogs bark. Colors seem crisper. The blue sky, the green grass are no longer fuzzy from the heat waves. Life returns.

You know how I said there is nothing like rain? Maybe I was mistaken. The more I think about it, tears are kind of like that. You are dealing with grief. Everything hurts. You feel helpless and hopeless. You think it will never end. Then, BOOM! You can't hold them back any longer. The tears flow. You fall to your knees. Your sobbing makes it difficult to draw a breath. Then the tears subside. Your breathing settles. You look up and see a friend, the sun, your dog, or a pretty picture. You smile. You say to yourself, "It's going to be okay."

I have learned a few things about grieving. One is that you can't hide from it. You have to go through the process. You can delay it, but you will pay the bill at some point.

The second thing is: real men do cry. If you don't want to cry because other people will think you are weak, you are weak. You are more concerned about what others will think of you than taking care of yourself. Real men don't give a damn about what someone else thinks about them. If you are hurting over losing a loved one, cry. Real friends will quietly offer their shoulder. Tears, like rain, bring relief and hope for better times. Live, laugh, love.

June 3, 2015
More about crying: This is from an article by Lizette Borreli for the website medicaldaily.com:

1. Releases Toxins
Crying does not only mentally cleanse us, it can cleanse our body too. Tears that are produced by stress help the body get rid of chemicals that raise cortisol, the stress hormone.

2. Kills Bacteria
A good cry can also be a good way to kill bacteria. Tears contain the fluid lysozyme — also found in human milk, semen, mucus and saliva — that can kill 90 to 95 percent of all bacteria in just five to 10 minutes.

3. Improves Vision
Tears, made by the lacrimal gland, can actually clear up our vision by lubricating the eyeballs and eyelids. When the membranes of the eyes are dehydrated, our eyesight may become a little blurry. Tears bathe the surface of the eye.

4. Improves Mood
Tears can elevate our mood better than any antidepressant available. A 2008 study from the University of South Florida found crying can be self-soothing and elevate mood better than any antidepressant. The shedding of tears improved the mood of almost 90 percent of criers compared to the eight percent who reported crying made them feel worse.

5. Relieves Stress
A good cry can provide a feeling of relief, even if our circumstances still remain the same. Crying is known to release stress hormones or toxins from the body, and as a result, reduces tension. Martin believes crying is a healthier alternative to punching the wall or "stuffing your feelings," which can lead to physical health problems like headaches or high blood pressure. "Crying is a safe and effective way to deal with stress," he said. "It provides an emotional release of pent up negative feelings, stresses, and frustrations."

6. Boosts Communication
Crying can show what words cannot express, especially in a relationship. This is mostly seen when a person in the relationship is having a different reaction to a situation that isn't transparent until tears begin to show. For example, "Someone may be trying to play it cool, or hold it together, or be out of touch with emotions — that are suddenly apparent when one person starts to cry," April Masini, relationship expert and author, told Medical Daily in an email.
It is at the moment one person bursts into tears that the flow of the conversation shifts toward the emotional aspect the conversation was covering. Masini believes, "The crying can quell a fight, emphasize a point not gotten across in words, or simply underscore the importance of the feelings behind the dialogue."

A good cry or two can naturally heal us both physiologically and psychologically.
Trust me, if you lose your spouse, you will cry. Let it out; it's good for you.

June 4, 2015
Nothing can stop me now
I'm on the top of the world
I can face any challenge
Fight any foe

Bring it on, world
Give me your best shot
...not that, not my wife
Cancer?! Really?
I meant something like a car accident
Maybe break a leg skiing
A leaky water pipe
An unexpected bill
I mean, I can handle anything
Let's be reasonable
...not that, not my wife
Cancer?! Really?
You should give me time to prepare
That was a sucker punch
You're not playing fair
Take it back, you piece of shit
She can't die this young
Give me your best shot
...not that, not my wife
Cancer?! Really?
All right, let's make a deal
I'm begging, take it back
Me, me, throw your best at me
She didn't provoke you
It was me bragging
I should be your target
...not her, not my wife
Cancer?! Really?
You've taken her away
Now I'm on my knees
I'm on the ground
You've won this round
You made her sick
But your target was me
...not her, not my wife
Cancer?! Really?
This fight isn't over
I'll get back up
Yes, you took her away
But haven't won yet
If I could grab you by the throat
I'd choke you til you die
...not that, not my wife
Cancer?! Really?

<u>June 5, 2015</u>
In the deepest, darkest depth of night
I see a bright and guiding light
And in the throes of all my pain
I know that I will live again
The girl I loved has gone away
But I woke up again today
She was taken away by a wave
She did not want to lie in a grave
I know that one day I will sleep
Until then I have a promise to keep
When faced with her mortality
She bravely faced reality
She turned to me and took my hand
She said before I leave this land
There is something you need to do
Promise me you'll find someone new
You need someone in your life
I want you to find another wife
She may not be anything like me
Being with her will set you free
I know you didn't want me to die
But you can't sit in a corner and cry
Go enjoy the beauty God made
Sit under a palm tree's shade
Experience everything life has to give
I want you very much to live
Don't mourn the life we could have had
Don't spend your time being mad
Find a girl that makes you smile
Spend some time on a tropic isle
I do not want you to fall
Find a new love and give it your all
Until you find your own release
I pray this lady will bring you peace
I hope you find it in your heart
To find someone and make a new start

<u>June 6, 2015</u>
Life goes on. That's what they say. I still wake up every day. I still
eat, work, shop, and pet my dog. I look in the mirror and see the
same face. And yet, everything is different. My house is no longer

my home. My church no longer gives me comfort. My friends keep their distance.

I have talked to others who have lost their spouse and found new love. It seems this is a common occurrence. People know you as part of a couple. When half of the couple is gone, they don't know how to deal with the survivor. I lost Marie. I was fortunate to find new love shortly after her death.

Cynthia's ex-husband was living in her house in Florida, so she had decided to stay in Pennsylvania with me. I made the mistake of trying to incorporate my new love into existing relationships. I took her to card parties and other group activities in which Marie and I participated. Cynthia was there, trying her best to fit in. My friends saw a person sitting where Marie was supposed to sit.

My choices are to continue my life with my existing friends alone, or move and start over with Cynthia. I am not meant to be alone and I love Cynthia, so there really is no choice. I know we will be moving soon. More than likely we will be heading south, away from snow.

She has two married daughters, Cheryl and Jillian, and four grandchildren. They have been very open and welcoming to me. Cheryl is a Penn Stater, which gives us common ground.

June 7, 2015
Wake up, get moving, we've got things to do
Time for dinner, another day done
Put an X on the calendar, this day is through
Wake up, get moving, we've got things to do
Time for church, another week done
Put an x on the calendar, this week is through
Wake up, get moving, we've got things to do
Time for Labor Day, another month done
Put an x on the calendar, this month is through
Wake up, get moving, we've got things to do
Time for Christmas, another year done
Put an x on the calendar, this year is through
Now it's time to reflect, to look back
What did I do this year, this month, this week, this day?
Did I accomplish anything worthwhile, lasting?
Did I make a difference in the world, in a single life?
What was so important it had to get done that day?

Did I take time to smell a rose, plant a tree, or say, "Have a nice day"?
We are here for each other, to be kind to our brother
Remember, we are not promised tomorrow
So, my advice for each day is: make it count

June 8, 2015
Love can't be measured
In ounces or a pound
It should be treasured
When it is found
Search high and low
with hope anew
but I hope you know
It's best when it finds you
You have a dream lover in mind
Maybe she has long hair
She has to be kind
She has to care
You hope she likes dogs
And is good with kids
Likes fireplace logs
And needs help with lids
Then one day, walking down the street
Your dream will appear
And you finally meet
The girl who brings cheer
You smile once more
You hear laughter again
Life is no longer a chore
And you are the envy of men
You go out on a date
In the shivering cold
It is never too late
You are never too old
You have to take a chance
Don't be afraid
Ask her to dance
You might make the grade
Pursue happiness
With all of your might
Anything less
Just wouldn't be right
Don't sit and cry

Don't scream and shout
Don't always ask why
Just get out and about
You'll pass the test
Find a new love
And give her your best
With help from above

June 9, 2015
More eye surgery tomorrow.....fun, fun, fun.
A few years ago, I had surgery to repair a torn retina. Four more
eye surgeries followed. I'm not a fan of surgery, though I've had
my share. It's mostly the needles and the IVs that bother me as I
am asleep through most of them.

I say "most of them" because I started coming out of anesthesia
in the middle of the latest surgery. When I discussed it with the
doctor, he brushed it off as no big deal. Maybe no big deal to him
but when you wake up to people messing with your eyes, it kind
of freaks you out a little.

June 10, 2015
Still Here
Marie is still here
day after day, year after year
when I see my children smile
hill after hill, mile after mile
when I see a flower
minute after minute, hour after hour
whenever I see a bunny
I still think of my honey
she will always be a part of me
like the Earth and Sky and Sea
I am with a new lady now
we were brought together somehow
we fit like a hand in a glove
and we're happy because
Marie taught me how to love.

June 11, 2015
When I was a young adult, my father had a video camera. He took
it on every vacation and chronicled many precious moments with
it. I borrowed it for one of my vacations.

After a few hours, I noticed that I was seeing only what I could see through the lens of the camera. I decided that, while documenting things is nice, I wanted to fully experience the moment, to see the big picture. I guess it's because I'm a stop-and-smell-the-roses kind of guy.

What's my point? I look at kids (and many adults) today who spend their lives bent over staring at their phones, thinking that Facebook is life. I like Facebook and use it as a tool. It allows me to express opinions and stay in touch with a wide array of friends. I do not live on Facebook. Use it, enjoy it, however, occasionally put it down, go get some sun, and smell some flowers. Live, laugh, love.

June 12, 2015
If you are reading this book, you have experienced grief. You may have lost a grandparent, parent, sibling, spouse, or, God forbid, a child. Each of these losses, in my experience, affects us in different ways.

I lost my last grandmother when I was in college. We were not close, as we lived five hours apart. To me, it was no big deal. Grandparents are supposed to die.

I was 40 when my dad died. That rocked me. I think it was the first time I faced my own mortality.
When Marie died, a part of me died with her. I lost not only her but friends and family as well. My siblings and my children are all still here and are healthy, thank God. I have had enough experience with death and grieving for a while.

My point is that grief is an individual experience. I have seen people bury their father and go to work the next day. Some people lose their spouse and lose their will to live, grieving until they too die. Some people are helped by being surrounded by friends, others seek solitude. Many people seek counseling and many others find solace in prayer. My healing was part prayer and part writing.

How will you heal? I don't know because we are all different. Whatever loss you are grieving, I pray you will find comfort and the will to go on and live your life.

<u>June 13, 2015</u>

I have always said that I know I am not the first to feel grief. I have also said that we all experience it in our own way. That being said, many people grieving share similar feelings.

I heard a song and marveled that the writer knew my heart so well. It is "Jealous of the Angels" by Jenn Bostic. Here are the lyrics:

I didn't know today would be our last
Or that I'd have to say goodbye to you so fast
I'm so numb, I can't feel anymore
Prayin' you'd just walk back through that door
And tell me that I was only dreamin'
You're not really gone as long as I believe
There will be another angel
Around the throne tonight
Your love lives on inside of me,
And I will hold on tight
It's not my place to question,
Only God knows why
I'm just jealous of the angels
Around the throne tonight
You always made my troubles feel so small
And you were always there to catch me when I'd fall
In a world where heroes come and go
Well God just took the only one I know
So I'll hold you as close as I can
Longing for the day, when I see your face again
But until then
God must need another angel
Around the throne tonight
Your love lives on inside of me
And I will hold on tight
It's not my place to question
Only God knows why
I'm just jealous of the angels
Around the throne tonight
Singin' hallelujah
Hallelujah
Hallelujah
I'm just jealous of the angels
Around the throne
Tonight

<u>June 14, 2015</u>
The Train
As I traverse this journey called grief, I am learning. I am learning about myself, my family, and my friends. I am learning about life, love, forgiveness, acceptance, and grief.

When I began this journey, I selfishly believed it was a solo journey. As I contemplate what I've learned about grief, I think of a train. Far from being alone, there are many passengers on this train. We are told that grief has five stages; denial, anger, bargaining, depression, and acceptance. These stages can be stations where people get off the train and spend some time. While we are all on the same train, we are not following a set schedule. Some people may linger at the anger station while others push on to spend some time bargaining. Others may go back to denial and start over again.

All of that is okay. As I said, there are many of us on this journey; however, we must take it at our own pace. I am finding that my journey is made better when I am more sensitive to the stages of my fellow travelers. I only wish Marie could have known the man I am becoming.

<u>June 15, 2015</u>
Anniversaries
We are quickly approaching what I expect will be a very difficult time for me (and others). As each day passes, I remember in great detail what happened on that date last year. Last July, I went on a mission trip to Tennessee with our church youth group. Marie asked me not to go, as she did each time I went away for a week to do God's work. "Everything is fine," I told myself. "One week away won't hurt anything."

I won't recount details of the weeks that followed. As I go through the next couple of months, I will look at the calendar and relive all of the pain and torment. Such is grief. If you happen to see me and I am crying, don't search for words, just offer your shoulder. If I see you crying, I will do the same. Live, laugh, love.

<u>June 16, 2015</u>
One woman, one man
I'll put a ring on her finger
And a braid in her hair
Yes, I'm going to linger

I'll always be there
She gives me hope
and helps me to cope
with all life has to give
one woman, one man
that's how I want to live
In this thing we call life
When I have to struggle
When I deal with strife
To have someone to snuggle
Helps me to cope
With all life has to give
One woman, one man
That's how I want to live.
As I walk down the long road
With burdens my own
I carry a heavy load
But I'm not alone
Cause she helps me to cope
with all life has to give
one woman, one man
that's how I want to live
As I'm growing older
And my goal is in reach
She leans on my shoulder
As we walk on the beach
And we help each other cope
with all life has to give
one woman, one man
that's how I want to live

June 17, 2015
Blue
The world now has a different hue
Even happy days have a hint of blue
Life goes on as you recover
From the loss of your lover
People smile and pat you on the back
It's not sympathy they lack
It is understanding
How can they know what you're going through
Their world is not colored blue
Though they are aware of Death
They weren't close enough to feel His breath

How can they know
When your tears don't show
It's bottled up inside
Good friends are few
When your world turns blue
They don't know what to say
When they come your way
They treat you like a stain
Not wanting to feel your pain
You are on your own
It is hard to start anew
When your world is tinged blue
You do the best you can
As a lonely, lonely man
Hoping in the coming days
The sun's rays
Will wash away the blue

June 18, 2015
Some days are tough
That's true enough
How will I get through
When all I see is blue
I still don't know why
She had to die
We were almost in our golden years
Now my days are filled with tears
We were going to savor
The fruits of our labor
We could both retire
And rekindle love's fire
We would spend our days and nights
Traveling, seeing new sights
Get in the camper and drive
Make a new home wherever we arrive
Ride the road til it ends
Make some new friends
Unfortunately we would find
God had something else in mind
Marie, you have cancer
And the doctors have no answer
Jesus came to take her home
And now alone I roam
Being a Christian man

I trust that God has a plan
He won't leave me when I am in pain
He'll show me how to live again
Plans will have to be adjusted
God still has to be trusted
I have a few more good years
With Him I have no fears
And when I cry
My tears He will dry

June 19, 2015

Summer is full of life. It is filled with bright colors. Green grass, blue skies, and flowers of every hue greet your eyes daily. Summer is noisy with birds chirping, bugs buzzing, and firecrackers marking celebrations.

If you closed your eyes and covered your ears, your nose would tell you it's summer: the varied scents from flowers blooming, farmers fertilizing, and manly men cooking on charcoal would shout, "Summer!"

Fall is filled with majestic colors and sharp scents. It is also filled with foreboding. Flowers and leaves disappear. Cold weather is coming. Winter is a different story. Winter is colorless, everything shades of grey or white. It is also quiet. The animals have gone south or are sleeping. People stay indoors, hiding from the cold. Winter smells are muted by the cold. Spring is a time of new hope and new life. Color returns as flowers and trees bloom. People venture outside again and look forward to summer.

The seasons are a kind of metaphor for the grieving cycle. Summer is when life is going good. Fall is when someone you love is dying. Winter is full-on grief. Your senses are numb. Everything turns grey. The world is cold and humorless. You have no appetite. When you walk, it feels like you are trudging through deep snow. Spring is when your grief is lifting. Colors return. Hope returns. You realize that your life, though changed, goes on.

June 20, 2015

Part of my journey has been seeing what others say about grief. Going through it, one wonders how long does this last? Will it always hurt like this? Is there some cure? Here are three thoughts on the subject:

"Grief is in two parts. The first is loss. The second is the remaking of life."
-- Anne Roiphe

"The hardest part of losing someone isn't having to say goodbye, but rather learning to live without them, always trying to fill the void, the emptiness that's left inside your heart when they go." Unknown

"Grief is not a disorder, a disease, or a sign of weakness. It is an emotional, physical and spiritual necessity, the price you pay for love. The only cure for grief is to grieve." -- Earl Grollman

June 21, 2015

I need to spend some time on my knees. I will start by asking for forgiveness (for what is between me and Him). Then I will ask Him to heal my broken heart. I will thank Him for the many ways He has blessed my life. Then I will ask for direction. Where do you need me, Lord? What do you want me to accomplish? How can I best serve others?

I need to spend some quiet time listening. Throughout my life, I (like the Israelites) have been close to God and have strayed from God. He has never strayed from me. He has never stopped loving me. He has never stopped blessing me.

People may ask, "How can you say that after losing your wife to cancer?" I don't know why she had to suffer or why she died so young. I do know that we will all die sometime. I do know that at the times I hurt the most, I felt His comforting presence the strongest. I don't know how I could go through this without my faith and my faith family.

June 22, 2015
The Lord is My Shepherd
The last several months have been terribly stressful for me. I know a little about stress from a stress management course I took several years ago. There are minor stressors like running late for work, not being able to find your keys, or just dealing with stupid people. Then there are major stressors like divorce, death of a parent, loss of a job, or death of a spouse. I am dealing with two of those and am not always able to remain my usual non-worrying self.

Last week in church, I was standing in the foyer waiting to help serve communion. I glanced at a picture on the wall. It was a pastoral painting with the words of the 23rd Psalm: "The Lord is my shepherd, I shall not want…"

I started feeling a sense of calm as I have always put my trust in Him. Another line in the Psalm is… "he leadeth me beside still waters." Today, our IU class took a field trip. Part of it involved a short hike down a hill to a landing beside a wide, shallow creek. It was so beautiful, peaceful, and calming. God is still speaking. He is telling me that everything will be okay. Peace be with you.

June 23, 2015
I am sitting here looking at my college ID from my freshman year at Penn State. I see a 17-year-old with tinted aviator glasses and shoulder-length hair. He is also skinny and kind of cocky-looking.

The kid in the picture met Marie about a year before he started college. He thought he would go to college, meet someone new, and Marie would be history. He had no idea that he would spend the next 40 years with her. It took four years of being apart and seeing each other on occasional weekends and summers for him to realize they were meant to be together.

It's funny the things you remember. That picture shows my hair at its longest length ever. I remember getting it cut the next day. It's also funny how time slips away. When I look at the picture, 40 years disappear. I remember the anxiety of being a freshman on a huge campus. I remember how I thought I was so much smarter than my parents (I wasn't). And, I remember being in love for the first time. It seems like yesterday.

They say when you die your whole life plays before your eyes. I don't think I'm going to die soon but when I look at this picture, scenes from our life together are replayed. Our first kiss, our wedding day, our first apartment, the time she bought a car without me, our kids being born and growing up, my son playing football, my daughter getting married, and Marie's illness and eventual death all flash by in an instant. How did 40 years go by? It doesn't seem like that long. I remember my parents dropping me off at my dorm; the next thing I know I'm writing this book.

Willie Nelson sure got it right: "Gee, ain't it funny how time slips away?"

June 24, 2015
If this hadn't happened
Who would I be
Everything I've been through
Made me me
Each new experience
Be it happy or sad
Changes us
For good or for bad
We can't live in a bubble
We all get nicks and scrapes
Every life has a few
Narrow escapes
How would you know joy
If you never felt despair
How would you know peace
If you never had a care
We are who we are
Because of where we've been
We know what we know
Because of what we've seen
My favorite dog scratched me
On my arm
Now I think of him
When I see the scar
Every little thing
That causes us to hurt
Makes us who we are
Like a sculptor shaping dirt
You can't hide
From a world full of pain
If you want to live a life
That's full again
Live your life
Without fear
Knowing that Death
Is always near
Find a reason to laugh
The world can be funny
Learn to enjoy the rain
It can't always be sunny
When you find love
Love with all your heart
You never know when you will part

<u>June 25, 2015</u>
Literature is full of metaphors. One popular subject for
metaphors is the butterfly.

The caterpillar is normal life. The caterpillar spends his time
eating, drinking, and working. He has no cares and doesn't think
about tomorrow. At some point, he decides to take a break. He
weaves a cocoon and spends some time chilling. After a while, he
breaks out of the cocoon and emerges as a butterfly.

Life and grief are kind of like that. You go through life, eating,
drinking, and working. You get lulled into a sense that life as we
know it will go on and on. Then, someone close to you is
suddenly gone. You experience grief. You go numb and hide from
the world. You trudge through each day, not tasting the food you
eat, not caring if your socks match, not wanting to be around
people.

As time passes, sunshine returns. You learn to smile again. You
have also learned a priceless lesson. Life is short and tomorrow is
not guaranteed. With this knowledge, you are a better person and
will make a better partner to a new love. You can't go back and
change the past. You were an ugly caterpillar. You can change the
future by using your new found wisdom and be a beautiful
butterfly.

<u>June 26, 2015</u>
Sometimes
Sometimes I feel like it's all been done
the race was lost before it was begun
the deck was stacked
the computer was hacked
the outcome was known
before I was grown
throw a dart at the wall
take a walk down the hall
everyone stares
nobody cares
why try
just cry
I don't
I won't
I will keep on trying
til the day I am dying

the fight is still in me
cross my path and you'll see
I will climb steep hills
I will tilt at windmills
I will firmly stand my ground
until the final victory is found.

June 27, 2015
I look forward to the day when Marie and I meet again in Heaven.
She will be there with her parents and my father. The only
emotions that we will feel will be love and joy. There will be no
tears and no need for apologies. We will join the ranks of
Heavenly beings worshipping God. We will also be waiting for
Cynthia to join us. Marie will welcome her with open arms.

June 28, 2015
When My Time Has Come
When my time here on Earth is done
I do not want your tears
Crying does not express who I was
Laugh and sing and dance
Play some music with the volume up high
Put on some Grateful Dead, followed by Willie
And then mellow out with some John Denver and James Taylor
Burn what's left of me and put me in the sea
Want a place to remember me? Plant a tree
Want to honor my memory? Volunteer
Feed the homeless in a soup kitchen
Help someone rebuild after a storm
Teach a child how to read
I've done all that and more
Not to brag or seek Earthly reward
But to do my small part to leave a better world
I'll never be famous
Who needs paparazzi chasing them around?
But I hope I've made a difference in at least one person's life

June 29, 2015
Looking Back
I took some time today to look back on some Facebook posts
from last year. I would like to share some from friends who
supported me during Marie's battle with cancer:

Dear God,
Please hold Marie, Dave & family in your loving arms.... comfort them &
give them courage to get thru these trying times.....one day at a time. Keeping
all if you in my prayers for a miracle. Love & hugs to all of you.
Keep the faith, God will lead you in the right direction. He'll be with you in
this trying time. Our prayers are to give strength and patience during this
time.

Hoping everything goes ok, Prayers going out to both of you.

Good Luck to your Better Half Dave, I hope everything works out for her.

Praying your meetings went well and you both came away psyched and
positive!!!!

Lots of prayers being said for you and your family. If you need anything
don't hesitate to ask!

I'm glad she's home. I'm sure she is much more comfortable at home. You just
can't get any sleep in a hospital!

Prayers for strength. So sorry you are going through this, no one should have
to. Thinking of all of you every hour.

As you can see, almost all mentioned prayer. I have always
believed that if you want to get to know someone, look at his
friends. Most of my friends are faithful believers. If you want to
strengthen your faith, surround yourself with faithful people.

In my search of Facebook posts, I also compiled comments made
about Marie shortly after she passed away.

June 30, 2015
Still Looking Back

A great sister-in-law and aunt, but most of all a good friend who never met a
stranger. She fought a good fight. A big loss for all of us who loved her, but
heaven's gain. We will remember her always.
We are so very sorry Dave, your beautiful girl is resting in the comforting
arms of Jesus. Prayers for you and your family...

We believe for these times! The cancer is gone, any pain is gone; she is starting
the next stage of eternity! You and your family are in our thoughts and
prayers

I am so very sorry you have to go through this. She was such a beautiful woman and lovely personality. I'll always remember her love for sandals . Love you Dave

I am so sorry to hear this Dave especially since I just found out last week what was going on with Marie. Heaven got an angel and I remember way back when u 2 got married and try to cherish those happy times. U take care and my deepest sympathy to u and your family. God Bless

We are very sorry for your loss Dave, but take comfort that Marie's pain and suffering are now gone and that she is at rest with God.

So sorry Dave! I will cherish all the memories of her smile and especially the good times we had on the cruises to Bermuda! Prayers are sent to you and family!

There are just no words, Dave......however I would like to say that you were AMAZING.....I never witnessed such a caring spouse and it was beyond heartwarming....thank you for taking care of my friend in such a gentle way for her last 107 days on this Earth and you guided her peacefully to heaven for eternity where she will sit by a lake and wait for us to arrive some day! Love you

There were some bumpy roads in her life. I miss her as much today as Ever!

I miss her so ......and always will
I still don't believe it's real. I know she has been watching over our baby the last few months.

She loved the bunnies and was always excited when they came and called me with joy. "The bunnies are here. The bunnies are here!" I will never see another bunny real or pretend without hearing her voice say,"The bunnies are here!"

She was always there to give me advice. She was always there to listen. She was always there to share her smile, her laugh, and her love. Marie used to always tell me that I was the best birthday present she ever got... Today I am missing her so much. the three of you are in my thoughts. Happy birthday to the best God mother anyone could ever ask for. We all miss you so much.

She was loved, and she is and will be missed by many.

I found this anonymous poem and found it lined up with where I
am in the grief process.

There is another side of grief
Where the tears still flow
Not as often
Where memories bring smiles
Not just sadness
Where blessings are recognized
Not as struggles
Where joy and peace are present
Not just sorrow
Where you are remembered
Not just mourned.

Early on in the grief process, a photo, a familiar scent, a favorite
location will bring on crushing pain and tears. As time goes on,
those same triggers will bring memories and smiles. Keep the
faith.

July 2, 2015
Pills
Have a headache? Take a Tylenol. Sprained your ankle? Take an
Aleve. Want to lose weight? There's a pill for that. Pregnant and
don't want to be? There's a pill for that. Nervous, seasick, have a
heart condition? There's a pill for that. Grieving? There are no
pills for that.

As I have said, the only cure for grieving is to grieve. Cry, punch
walls, spend days in bed. Do whatever your body tells you to do.
Don't fight it. Don't try to hide from it. Don't try to deny it. And,
don't take pills to mask it. You are hurting. You are supposed to
hurt. Go with it. Ride it out. The only cure is time. You will
recover. Your life will go on. Sunshine and joy will return.

July 3, 2015
I have often heard married couples sniping at each other, usually
over trivial things. You left toast crumbs on the table. You left
your bra hanging on the door. Your friends are obnoxious. You
never buy me flowers. We never have sex anymore.

I always think to myself, there was a day that these people loved
each other so much they got married. What happened? Okay,

familiarity breeds contempt. But there is more to it than that. I think they forgot their vows. You know, "For better or worse?" Marriage is tough. You have to work at it. You have to put blinders on to hide your spouse's flaws while celebrating her special qualities.

You also have to remind yourself that one day, one of you will die and the other will be left with only memories. When that happens, you forget all the bad things and remember only those special qualities. When that happens, you wish you could go back and do it over, do it right. Unfortunately, in life, there are no do-overs. Unfortunately, in life, some lessons are learned too late. Maybe some smart person out there will learn from my mistake and buy his sweetheart some flowers.

July 3, 2015
You Can't Keep A Good Man Down
I won't go through life wearing a frown
I've lost my dear Marie
But it won't be the end of me
There's still life ahead
I won't spend it in bed
I'm not done crying
But I'm not yet dying
I've got too much to do
I can't sit and be blue
Don't be mad
That I don't appear sad
You can't know what is in my heart
My pain can't be graphed on a chart
I'll continue to grieve
But won't wear my heart on my sleeve
On this I won't budge
It's not your place to judge

July 4, 2015
Happy birthday, America!

July 5, 2015
Every day is an adjustment. Losing your spouse knocks your whole life out of whack. When you lose someone who has been beside you for 40 years, you have to start over, relearn everything. In the first hours, you forget how to breathe. It feels like you are

being waterboarded and you gasp for breath. You forget how to walk. You just slump down into a chair and sit. You forget how to smile and laugh. You forget how to feel anything except pain. You forget how to talk as your mind is a jumbled mess. You forget how to sleep, partly because you're not used to sleeping alone and partly because your mind won't shut up.

As time passes, you start to breathe again. You get up out of the chair and walk again. You see a baby and smile again. Someone tells a joke and you laugh again. You still feel pain but you find room for other feelings as well. Your mind settles into the new reality and allows you to communicate again. Whether it is exhaustion or the fact that your mind finally shuts up, you are able to sleep again. Memories that once brought tears now bring smiles.

I will never forget Marie. I will never get over losing Marie. I will go on with my life and I will love again. They say it is better to have loved and lost than never to have loved. I guess you could also say it is better to have loved and grieved than never to have loved. Grief and love are intertwined. You will not grieve someone you never loved. Lots of people died when I was growing up but I never knew grief until my father died. Even that experience did not prepare me for losing Marie.

July 6, 2015
Walk along with me
My beautiful Marie
Share my life
Be my wife
We will be together
From now until forever
We will raise a girl and a boy
In a home filled with joy
We'll save our money
For someday, Honey
When we can retire
And sit by a fire
We'll talk about how lucky we are
To have gotten this far
Then something went wrong
She didn't live that long
Plans were changed
My life rearranged

Now it's just me
And she is now free
Her pain is ended
My life upended
Somehow I will find
Some peace of mind
I'll make a new start
And mend my broken heart

July 7, 2015
Where does love go when life comes to an end
Where does it go
We who are left can only pretend
Does anyone really know
My pastor told me
It's off to Heaven she went
Can anyone see
What he really meant
We like to believe
There is something beyond
It's hard to conceive
That gone is just gone
She is at peace
She's gone to her rest
She didn't just cease
I need someone to attest
I have to know
Is she up above
Please tell me so
That surrounded by God's love
She is looking down
A smile on her face
No reason to frown
Because of God's grace

July 8, 2015
Kintsugi
Did you ever drop a ceramic cup or vase and watch it shatter into
pieces? Did you get out the Elmer's glue and try to repair it? At
best, the vessel is never quite the same. It is missing small pieces
and the cracks are painfully obvious. After attempting repair, the
once beautiful object is discarded.

Another option is Kintsugi. Kintsugi is a centuries old Japanese tradition of repairing ceramic vases using gold. The translation is "golden joinery." The idea is to fit the broken pieces back together and fill the remaining cracks with gold. The result is a vessel more beautiful than the original.

I was on a Christian retreat a few years ago. During the closing ceremonies, we broke ceramic pots to symbolize our brokenness. After the ceremony, I spoke to the leader of the retreat. I asked if he had heard of Kintsugi. He had not.

I explained the process to him I then told him that being a born-again Christian is rather like Kintsugi. Yes, we are broken but when we are born again, we are made whole and even more beautiful than before. We are the shattered pots. God's love is the gold that makes us new.

July 9, 2015
Some say my angel watches over me
How can that possibly be?
In Heaven there are no tears
If she's watching, she'll see my fears
Someone is lying
She'll see me crying
How could she know joy
Knowing her man has become a little boy
Does she only see the happy days
When I am warmed by the Sun's rays
Does god block her view
When I am feeling blue
I don't want her watching me
I want her to be free
She paid her Earthly dues
Let Heaven sadness refuse
Let her only feel love
In her eternity above

July 10, 2015
I am a man with two hearts. One is broken and aching from the loss of my dear Marie. The other is bursting with joy over my new found love, Cynthia. How can both hearts beat inside the same chest? How can pain live beside joy? I guess it is like yin and yang, good and evil balancing each other.

My older friends are still hurting and (I guess) expect me to still be hurting. They seem to have a hard time accepting that I have found new love and am happy. My newer friends never knew Marie and don't understand how I can be sad when I am in love. To be honest, I haven't got it all figured out myself. I'm just taking it one day at a time.

July 11, 2015
Marie was shy and quiet, usually content to be in the background. She was also a very strong, intelligent, and creative woman. She loved doing things to make other people smile, though she rarely smiled herself. Her depression robbed her of the happiness she deserved. I tried to help her and to get her help. She preferred to tough it out. Being an optimist and generally happy person, I could not understand her depression. In a bit of irony, losing her and experiencing grief, I now can relate to her sadness.

July 12, 2015
Balance
It's all about balancing things in your life. If you want to eat rich foods, be prepared to balance it with exercise. If you don't, you'll get fat. If you want to skydive, you better pack and check your parachute. If you don't, you'll get flat. If you want to go on fancy vacations, you have to work hard the rest of the year or you'll go broke. If you want to fry a turkey, keep a fire extinguisher handy or you'll go up in smoke. I have to somehow find a balance between grieving my lost wife and being happy about my new found love.

July 13, 2015
No one knows the day or hour
When they will meet the higher power
Though we know
One day we will go
You and me, my friend
Will both come to an end
Will we grow old and gray
Who is to say
Or will we die young
With some many things undone
Will we die in an accident
Or succumb to a life misspent
One day, loved ones will draw near
Our final wishes to hear

We will have to make peace
With the idea that our life will cease

July 14, 2015
A picture in my wallet
Is all that I have now
Of the girl
That I kissed upon her brow
We said our goodbyes
About a year ago
How I am still standing
I will never know
She left so suddenly
There was no time to adjust
If I am to go on
In God I have to trust
He took my wife away from me
And took away our kids' mother
Somehow we'll have to find a way
To comfort and strengthen each other
Day after day I still cry
My eyes like a leaky faucet
When I look at the girl
On the picture in my wallet

July 15, 2015
Get in your car. Back out of your driveway. Now, keep it in
reverse and drive looking in the rearview mirror. How did that go?
Probably not well.

Life is the same way. You can't live your life looking back. I am
not saying that lost loved ones should be forgotten. I will never
forget Marie. That being said, I have a new life now, full of hope
and possibilities. Marie knew she was going to die and did not
want me to be alone. I can best honor her memory by being
happy with my new love.

July 16, 2015
Once there was a young boy
With a promise of life ahead full of joy
Then he met a young girl
That set his heart in a whirl
In a short while, they said I do
Everyone knew

They would be together
Forever
They built a home
Where two kids would roam
They worked and slaved
Every nickel they saved
For the day in the future
When they would be secure
Then something went awry
That gave them reason to cry
I'm leaving you, she said
For soon I will be dead
He did not believe it
He could not conceive it
Then on a dark and dreary day
Her words came true, she went away
And left a sad old man
Who had no plan
On how to make a new start
With a badly broken heart

July 17, 2015
My dear Marie
How could it be
That you are no longer here
I gave you my heart
And said til death do us part
Not really knowing what that meant
I fell in love with you
with your eyes of blue
and your long blond hair
then cancer took you away
on that cold winter day
leaving me so all alone

July 18, 2015
Young people believe they will live forever
Only old people die
Young people think, "That will happen to me never."
They don't even know it's a lie
I can drink and smoke
I'll never get cancer
I'll just take a toke
That's the answer

I can drive really fast
Get out of my way, old man
I've got to get past
That's my plan
Every day seek a new thrill
Maybe jump out of a plane
Only old people chill
Sitting still makes me insane
Then one day
Some kid calls you old
You say, "No way!"
But notice you are cold
You make noise when you stand
And if you should stumble
You are careful how you land
As you might break something in the tumble
Your joints start to ache
Though you've done no harm
And the candles on your cake
Set off the alarm
How can this be
I was young last week
Now I can't see
And my joints creak
Somehow I got old
I don't know why
I was so bold
Does this mean I'm going to die?

July 19, 2015

I lost someone close to me. She died last year. Now I am alone. She is no longer here.

No, that's wrong. Thirty some years ago, we decided to marry. Our wedding bulletin said, "And two shall become one." We did. We became one.

She is still here. She is a part of me. She will always be with me. Though at times I may be lonely, I will never be alone. In quiet times, I will hear her voice, see her smile, and gaze into her blue eyes. Even after I am gone, she will still be here. She will be with our two children, our family, and our friends.

July 20, 2015
Please hold me close, dear Lord. Comfort me in my grief. For death has come like a thief.
He has stolen our future and destroyed our dreams. Now my life is coming apart at the seams.

I was supposed to go first, that was my plan. Now I'm just doing the best that I can. If only I could go back and do it again. I'd get it right this time, just tell me when.

July 21, 2015
A little bird showed up when I was grilling in the rain. He looked a little upset about getting wet, so I picked him up and moved him to a dry spot. I have always had a way with animals.

July 22, 2015
Beautiful Bird
Yesterday, I was cooking dinner on the grill. I put the food on and went back in the house. As often happens this time of year, an afternoon rain shower began. When I went out to check the food, I noticed a bird sitting next to the grille. She seemed upset because the storm caught her off guard and she was unable to fly with wet wings. I introduced myself and assured her I would not harm her, in fact, I would try to help her.

I approached slowly so as not to spook her. She made no protest when I offered to pick her up and take her to a sheltered area of the porch. When the rain stopped, she had to dry her feathers so we took some time to get to know each other. I picked her up again and moved her into a sunny spot where she could warm up and dry her wings. The thought briefly crossed my mind that I could keep her as a pet. Beautiful birds however are meant to be free, she could not stay.

I checked on her several times, wondering if she was injured and would require nursing. The third time I checked, she had flown away. I will probably never see her again. We did share some special time together. I have memories and pictures as proof. Instead of being sad, I will rejoice knowing she is where she is supposed to be.

Looking back on this post, I realize I may have been talking about Marie being where she is supposed to be.

July 23, 2015
God has blessed me in so many ways. That may seem like a
strange statement from someone who is grieving. However, if you
are a believer, you'll understand. When I am injured and forced to
use crutches, I thank God I can still walk.

A few years ago, I tore my retina. I underwent several surgeries
that left me with slightly blurred vision in that eye. I thank God I
can still see. I have always had a roof over my head and food on
my table. For that, I thank God. Yes, I lost my wife. We had 40
years together and for that, I thank God.

July 24, 2015
When Marie died, I was numb. I couldn't think. I couldn't see,
feel, or hear. How could this happen? Who can I blame? I still
have some tough days but I'm starting to live again.

July 25, 2015
I was angry with the physician's assistant that so cruelly delivered
the diagnosis. I was angry with the world renowned cancer expert
who led us to believe he could cure her. I was angry with the
insurance company for delaying treatment.

I have decided that if I am to live the life I was meant to live,
anger has no place. Being angry with someone does not hurt
them. It does hurt you. Carrying a grudge is tiring work that
serves no purpose. If you were involved and made me angry, I
forgive you.

July 26, 2015
Though I am in a forgiving mood, Cancer, I still hate you.

July 27, 2015
They say that grief is unpredictable. They got that right. Does it
last two weeks,, two years, or two decades? Who knows? Each
individual case is different. Do you ever stop grieving? Who
knows?

Each case is different. I think it starts out pretty much the same
for everyone. When someone close to you dies, it's like you got
the wind knocked out of you. You can't breathe, you can't think.
Then for a while, you go through the motions of living. After a
time, you start to smile again and think, "I'm going to be okay."
Then you hear a song or see a picture and you crumble again.

July 28, 2015

I know I'm repeating myself (please forgive me, I am still grieving and not always thinking clearly) but we played "Sweet Caroline" at Marie's memorial. Every time I hear it (which is a lot), I cry.

Several years ago, Eric Clapton lost his young son in an accident. He wrote "Tears in Heaven" to express his grief. Knowing the effect that "Sweet Caroline" has on me, I wonder how Eric can get through "Tears in Heaven" in a live performance. Eric, sorry for your loss and thank you for an amazing song.

July 29, 2015

My last post about Eric Clapton got me curious. I already looked up (and wrote) poetry about grief. Now I was wondering if there were other songs about grief. I shouldn't have wondered. Most songs are poems set to music and most poems express deep feelings. It only makes sense that there would be hundreds of songs dealing with grief.

One of my favorite songs is "Fire and Rain" by James Taylor. I always thought it was about his battle with depression. When I searched for songs about grief, I learned that he wrote it when dealing with the loss of a childhood friend. I also found a song by Diamond Rio called "One More Day," which expresses my feelings quite well. I see karaoke in my future.

July 30, 2015
Endings/Beginnings
Today was the last day of ESY camp ["extended school year" camp for special needs kids, where I have taught for three years] for this year. Each teacher or aide is assigned to be with one student for the entire camp. My student was a teen boy who was non-verbal but very strong-willed. With patience, I was able to communicate with him and we found a way to work together.

It was time to say goodbye to students and staff. I find it amazing how quickly you can become attached to someone who cannot speak. Three hours per day, four days per week, for four weeks and we figured out how to communicate with each other and accomplish things together. I will miss him. I was also fortunate to work with talented and caring staff members. I will miss them as well.

The end of ESY also marks the beginning of some painful anniversaries. Last August 1, Marie first complained of double vision. August 4, we were given her diagnosis. In two weeks, we will head to Canada for a final farewell. Please feel free to share pictures or memories of Marie as part of our healing process.

August 12, 2015

The Lighthouse
An island lighthouse
White with a red cross
Looking over the ocean wave
Dolphins splashing about
Eagles flying overhead
This does not look like a grave
Set me on fire
Put me in the sea
That was Marie's final wish
Not in the ground
No stone at my head
Allow me to swim with the fish
We went by boat
The captain unaware
Smuggled aboard was a stowaway
Marie in an urn of salt
Made to melt in the sea
We came to say goodbye today
Now aware of our plan
The captain said, Leave it to me.
We'll go on a whale watching tour."
He motored about
Salt spray in our face
And picked the perfect spot for sure
She wanted one thing
In her life
To make her happy would take
Just one thing
For me to say
We bought a house on a lake
She loved the beach
The Sun and sand
But mostly she loved the water
Now she's at peace
In a beautiful place
Put there by me, our son, and our daughter

In August of 2015, my son Brad, my sister-in-law Jane and I set off to visit my daughter Kristy in Canada. As per Marie's wishes, we'd had her cremated. Her final wish was to be cremated and then placed in the ocean. I believe cremation was her way of having a final victory over cancer. The fire would destroy the devil that destroyed her.

The beach had always been her favorite place. The beach was a place free of stress with the sound of the waves having a calming effect. She specified the Bay of Fundy as that would put her close to our daughter's home. Her remains had been placed in a salt urn, designed to dissolve when placed in water. The urn held a place of honor in our home for several months until we could make arrangements for the trip.

The three of us -- actually four if you count my dog -- took two days to drive to Canada. We crossed the border with our fingers crossed. In our car, we had a dog, a honey baked ham, bananas, slightly more beer than technically allowed (about double the legal amount), and Marie's remains. After a few routine questions and a few awkward responses on my part, we were waved through.

We spent a few days visiting with Kristy and her husband, Lucas. We played board games, hiked, drank, and reminisced. Lucas made arrangements to go whale-watching in the bay. It was only after we boarded the boat that we revealed the true purpose of the trip to the captain. He was very accommodating and said he had done this several times.

We spent a few hours tooling around the bay. We saw several whales, some dolphins, seals, and many water birds. At one point, the captain cut the motor, looked at me and asked if this spot was okay. I took a moment to take it in. He had stopped just a short way from Campobello Island, the horizon dominated by a beautiful lighthouse. I could not have chosen a better spot. Everyone was in agreement that Marie would approve.

We gathered together and said a few final words. I lifted the salt urn and leaned over the rail. I said, "I love you." I then released my love to the sea. The urn hit the water with a splash that soaked me. It was just Marie's way of saying goodbye. We all laughed. It was welcome relief to a somber moment. I estimate that with the currents, Marie has now traveled around the world.

PART SIX: LIFE GOES ON

I am writing this in July of 2017. Marie has been gone almost three years. I still miss her, but it no longer hurts when I think about her. I have gone through the grieving process and can now think of her and smile. We made many happy memories and time has clouded images of our struggles. I am still grieving, though.

In the process of finding new love and beginning a new life, I lost friends and family. People that knew Marie have not accepted Cynthia. People that never met Marie like Cynthia and see us as a great couple.

As much as losing lifelong friends hurts, what hurts most is how my relationship with my kids has changed. I am trying to keep in touch, but they both hate talking on the phone and rarely answer my calls. They occasionally respond to texts, though lately it takes longer if they respond at all. I am at a loss as to how to remedy this. What I do know is that Cynthia and I are enjoying our adventures and I hope we share many years together.

As time went on, I continued to post on Facebook, but less frequently:

September 30, 2015
Thirty-seven years ago, in a small church in Bath, Pennsylvania, we said, "I do." Last year, on our anniversary in our small house in Bath, Pennsylvania, we said, "I love you," kissed, and said goodbye.

November 17, 2015
Shortly after Marie passed away, someone (I do not recall who it was) gave me a printout of a story called "The Last Time," author unknown. Here it is:

From the moment you hold your baby in your arms
you will never be the same.
You might long for the person you were before,
When you have freedom and time,
And nothing in particular to worry about.
You will know tiredness like you never knew it before,
And days will run into days that are exactly the same,

Full of feedings and burping,
Nappy changes and crying,
Whining and fighting,
Naps or a lack of naps,
It might seem like a never-ending cycle.
But don't forget …
There is a last time for everything.
There will come a time when you will feed
your baby for the very last time.
They will fall asleep on you after a long day
And it will be the last time you ever hold your sleeping child.
One day you will carry them on your hip then set them down,
And never pick them up that way again.
You will scrub their hair in the bath one night
And from that day on they will want to bathe alone.
They will hold your hand to cross the road,
Then never reach for it again.
They will creep into your room at midnight for cuddles,
And it will be the last night you ever wake to this.
One afternoon you will sing "the wheels on the bus"
and do all the actions,
Then never sing them that song again.
They will kiss you goodbye at the school gate,
The next day they will ask to walk to the gate alone.
You will read a final bedtime story and wipe your last dirty face.
They will run to you with arms raised for the very last time.
The thing is, you won't even know it's the last time
Until there are no more times.
And even then, it will take you a while to realize.
So while you are living in these times,
remember there are only so many of them
and when they are gone, you will yearn for just one more day of
them.
For one last time.
While the subject is about parenting, the message applies to
spouses as well.
There is a last time you went out to dinner with her.
There is a last time you danced with her.
There is a last time you sat next to her in church, held her hand,
told her she was beautiful, ate her cookies, went to a movie with
her, wished her happy birthday, took a cruise with her, a last time
you kissed her. And, each last time, you did not realize it was the
last time. And, yes, you will yearn for one more last time.

<u>November 18, 2015</u>
One Year
A year has gone by
and I'm still asking why
She died so very young
leaving a daughter and a son
to find their way on their own
their father, their parent, left alone
She was so very smart
and touched many a heart
by simply being kind
she had that kind of mind
and she offered a listening ear
when someone was troubled with fear
Others always came first
even when she suffered the worst
and though she had a family
work was where she wanted to be
though she was their boss
for them it was a terrible loss
because in the end
she was their friend
Her friendships were strong
and lasted lifelong
they will always remember
this day in November
the sadness that it brings,
memories of the day when Marie got her wings.

Yes, it has been a year since we said goodbye to my brother-in-law,
John and my wife, Marie. It has been an amazing year. Certainly, I
have cried my share of tears and have many more to shed.
However I have also grown as a person, a father, and a friend. I
am learning patience, empathy, and a lot about love and
friendship.

Thankfully, I have not had to make this journey alone. Over the
year, people have offered shoulders to cry on, hugs, food,
companionship, or simply a listening ear. All of your kind words,
thoughts, and deeds are greatly appreciated. I thank my family, my
friends, and my new found love for helping me through this.
Better times are certainly ahead of us. Live, laugh, love!

59

59 and counting
I'm feeling quite young
but the years are mounting
the way I lived who'd have believed
I'd still be around
I should be very relieved
I'm not giving up on my dream
though distant at times
it may seem
one day I am going to teach
it's definitely a goal
I will one day reach
though Marie is no longer here
I know forever
she will be near
better children no one ever had
and no matter what happens
I am still their Dad
my friends ever true
will never allow me
to ever be blue
with Cynthia now by my side
my smile's returned
for the rest of the ride
I say this from the bottom of my heart
yes, it is true
I am officially an old fart.

July 27, 2016

The house that Marie and I built is empty. It has been sold and we are moving to South Carolina. I spent three years searching for a teaching job in Pennsylvania. I am convinced that God has other plans for me. Last month, I attended a job fair in South Carolina and received three job offers. I need a full-time job, I no longer enjoy snow, and I don't want to spend any more time in the house where Marie died. It is time to go.

About a year after her death, we experienced a 30-inch snowfall. That did it for me. Cynthia and I moved about an hour west of Myrtle Beach. This winter I saw a ten-minute snow flurry. That was the extent of our South Carolina winter. Works for me.

September, 2016
Cyn and I are adjusting to life in the South. People are warm and welcoming. Our neighbors have welcomed us with open arms. We are both happy to be involved in a community. While we miss the great restaurants and easy access to stores, we are only an hour from Myrtle Beach. You learn to take the bad with the good.

September 5, 2016
I was hired to teach fourth grade ELA and Social Studies. When school started, they moved me to fifth grade ELA. Two weeks in, they moved me to first grade. I will do my best; however, had I known, I would have accepted a different offer.

October 2016
I am now teaching first grade. After a rough start, I am adjusting. I was used to teaching fourth grade. First grade requires a different style and a different pace. The kids and I are learning something every day and we are both smiling more.

November 5, 2016
We are now approaching the second anniversary of Marie's death. I am still teaching first grade in South Carolina. I am quite busy and still haven't figured out how to get the students to buy into my teaching. Classroom disruptions are the norm, not the exception, and I get little support from administration. I am so frustrated.

December 21, 2016
I was sitting in the Myrtle Beach airport awaiting my flight to Pennsylvania. After earning of a delay, I overheard a college student talking to her mother on the phone. As I listened, I flashed back to conversations my kids had with their mom. When she ended the call, she said, exasperatedly, "I wish my mom would stop worrying."

I told her my wife drove my kids crazy with her worrying. Then I told her that she was no longer here and my kids would love to have her worrying over them again. I added, "Merry Christmas." She thought a moment, smiled, and said, "Merry Christmas to you, too." She then promised to give her mom a big hug when she got home.

176

I injured my ankle two years ago. I kept thinking it would get better. It hasn't. I went to a doctor and he recommended surgery. I tried to put it off until the end of the school year. Last Friday, the combination of the ankle pain and the stress of first year teaching became too much.

I resigned my teaching position. I may teach again after surgery, or I may retire. When asked, I tell people I am practicing for retirement. I am going to try it for a year and if I'm any good at it, I'll stick with it. The district is threatening to petition the state to pull my certificate for breach of contract. (The district has since relented, as it was a legitimate medical issue.) Come what may, I have learned to not waste my life doing something I do not enjoy.

If you are living, you are learning. I learn something new every day. I have learned that you can learn something from everyone you meet. As a teacher, I often learn from my students. I learned a valuable lesson from a girl with autism. She could not speak, other than making grunting noises. She was prone to temper tantrums where she would cry, pull her hair out in clumps, and try to strike anyone foolish enough to try to calm her. I was working with her, matching picture cards to words cards, picture of an apple on one, the word apple on another.

After going through the matching process the way she had always done it, on a whim, I decided to mix it up. I arranged the cards in different ways. I had assumed she was simply matching memorized images. As I tried each new arrangement, the girl quickly demonstrated that she was, in fact, reading. From that I learned not to limit any student by what they can't do and to try to find what they can do. I lost my wife to cancer. I went on the roller coaster ride we call grief. What have I learned from this experience?

I have learned that people and experiences are more important than money or things. Any time you spend chasing dollars to buy things is time you could have spent watching your child grow, enjoying the beauty of a sunset, or holding your wife's hand. This knowledge makes me much less likely to purchase things on an impulse. I find myself, in stores, asking myself, do I need this? More often than not, the answer is no. I have also begun working on decluttering. When you sell a house and move to another state, you really look at everything you own. You ask yourself, "Do I need this? When was the last time I used this? Does it hold deep sentimental meaning?" I sold or gave away many things that were just taking up space. My life is much less cluttered with things and much more centered on relationships and experiences.

I've learned that being selfish is costly. By being open and generous, you welcome people into your life. Being selfish closes doors and leaves you lonely. After I became more involved in my church, I started increasing my weekly offering. It seemed the more I gave, the less I worried about money.

When I donated my time as a Sunday School teacher, I discovered a passion and a new career. I gave my time, money, and talent to help lead mission trips, only to discover the unmatched joy that comes from helping others. If you want to be truly rich, give of yourself.

Sometimes we are to comfort others, sometimes we are to allow others to comfort us. This is kind of a paraphrase of the example that Jesus laid out for us when he washed his disciples' feet. One disciple tried to refuse his attempt to wash his feet. He said, "Master, I should wash your feet." Jesus told him if he did not allow him to wash his feet, he could not follow him. Sometimes we are to serve others, sometimes we are to allow others to serve us.

Think about it. If we are all always trying to serve, who will there be to serve? Allowing others to do things for us can be difficult and require swallowing some pride. Open yourself up. When you are hurting, accept hugs, let people cook for you. You will both be better for the experience. God has often put me in situations where it is clear that I am supposed to help. I was walking through a grocery store and saw a little old lady looking at an item on the top shelf, clearly out of her reach. Without a word, I plucked the item from the shelf and handed it to her. Her response, "I was praying for an angel to help me." I'm no angel but I know God put me there for her.

After my latest surgery, I could not walk for several weeks. I was concerned about how the grass would get cut. I was sitting on my couch and heard an engine in my front yard. My neighbor, knowing my situation, took it upon himself to cut my grass. My neighbor is retired military and a preacher. He talks the talk and walks the walk.

One of the hardest lessons I learned is that friendships can be fragile. Lifelong friends can disappear as circumstances change. Many of Marie and my friends never gave Cynthia a chance and no longer communicate with me. This loss of friendships is as painful as the loss of my wife. I am hopeful that one day the situation will change.

Grief is a process. It involves a series of steps. Though most people experience all or many of the steps, the time spent at each step varies widely. You can quarantine yourself and avoid people and reminders of your loss. At some point, you have to face it. You can drink or take pills to deaden the pain. At some point, you have to face it. You can put on a brave face and hold back the tears. At some point, you have to face it.

What worked for me was allowing myself to experience everything in the moment. There were moments of confusion. Why me? How could this happen to Marie? There were times of anger. Why didn't the doctors move more quickly? Did those two weeks of waiting ruin her chances? At times I felt helpless and overwhelmed. How would I go on without her? Could I maintain our lifestyle on my meager income? And there were plenty of tears. I cried unashamedly whenever and wherever I was.

Of course, I also wrote. During her illness, I was pretty much confined to the house and used Facebook to communicate with the outside world. After Marie died, it was just me and my dog. Rather than settling for one-sided conversations with a collie, I continued to use Facebook as a lifeline to my friends and family. Often, a line or two would pop into my head. I would rush to jot it down or quickly begin typing. Poems would flow freely, often without revision. As tears rid the body of toxins, the poems rid my soul of pain.

You do not have control over who you will love. I did not go to the skating rink believing I would find my bride-to-be. One glimpse of her, and I knew our futures would be locked together.

When I asked Cynthia to join me for dinner, I only intended for two lonely people to share a meal and comfort each other over our losses. At some point during the dinner, I realized that we would be spending some time together. I realized it before she did. We were listening to a Tim McGraw CD. One of the songs contains the line, "One of these days you're going to love me." As the song ended, I looked at her and said, "One of these days you're going to love me." It wasn't too long after that she conceded she had indeed fallen in love with me. I am very fortunate to have had the love of two women in my life.

I am very much in love with Cynthia and I am enjoying life once again. My children and my friends talk regularly, as they always have. Most of them are still, understandably hurting from losing Marie and are not ready to welcome someone new into the situation. I hope in time they will open their hearts.

Some people can strap on a backpack and head into the woods, content to be alone and one with nature for weeks at a time. That's not me. I am a social animal. I am not meant to be alone. Marie was even more aware of that fact than I was. Her first concern was not for herself but that I find someone for myself when she left. I think some of my family and friends would have preferred me staying a pitiable widower, wallowing in grief. I truly believe I would not have lasted long in such a state.

Cynthia and I have a friend who lost his wife to cancer several years ago. He is still single and still wallowing in his grief. That is his choice and his journey. Which is another lesson learned. We are all affected by and deal with grief in our own way, in our own time. You can't say one month isn't long enough or two years is too much time to grieve. It is an individual journey. The ride may be short and intense or excruciatingly long. It can't be rushed and there is no cure other than time. If you are hurting, let others know and accept their comfort. If someone you know is hurting, let them know you are there for them.

One of the most important lessons for me was the importance of faith. It is easy to be angry with God when things go bad. One can feel deserted and unloved by God. Some even question the existence of God when facing trials. I grew up in the Christian faith. I strayed for a bit, as most young adults do. At one point, I felt an emptiness that instinctively I knew was only to be filled with a relationship with God.

When our troubles began, my faith was strong. I leaned on God for comfort and understanding. At the darkest, loneliest times, I still felt a strong hand and saw a light in the distance guiding me to better times. It was these quiet times that allowed me to be still and to listen. The recurring message was: Things will be okay. You will be okay. Like most people, I do not understand how a loving God can allow suffering. Perhaps one day understanding will come. Until then, I am confident there is a God and He loves us like a parent loves a child.

Most books spend the last few pages wrapping up the story and bringing everything to a nice, neat end. Happy or sad, the story is over. That will not be the case for this book. I told you at the beginning that this was a book about life. While my life is closer to the end than the beginning, it goes on. I still receive inspiration and continue to write. I will close this volume with my latest poem.

On the Path
When you find yourself
On the path of pain and broken dreams
You may wonder
Is life really what it seems
We always think
There is going to be more
More time
More trips to the store
As the second hand
Sweeps the clock
Your friendships
Are your rock
Then you find your tether
Is no more
Than a feather
You pack your things
Load the car
And spread your wings
When you land
You dip your toes

And walk in sand
With someone new
To hold your hand
You find new ties
That make you smile
And if you are wise
With the new friends
You have found
You still hope
Old friends will come around

Live, Laugh, Love.

ADDENDUM: QUOTES ABOUT GRIEF

Obviously, I am not the first person to have experienced a loss. I am not the only person to ever go through a grieving process. Death has been with us from the start; each of us born to die.

Different cultures have different customs involving death and grief. We wear black, have viewings and funerals, cry, and leave the widow/widower to go on with their lives. Other cultures have prescribed rituals. Some prohibit music, others encourage it. Some say grieving should last 40 days, others say it should go on for one year.

While I have learned that grief is an individual thing and we all experience it and cope with it in different ways, there are some universal truths. Death touches each of us -- it is one sure thing in every life. In writing this book, I wondered, what do others say about grief? The following passages helped me.

The first two tell us that we can get on with our lives but we are forever changed.

"The reality is that you will grieve forever. You will not 'get over' the loss of a loved one; you will learn to live with it. You will heal and you will rebuild yourself around the loss you have suffered. You will be whole again but you will never be the same. Nor should you be the same nor would you want to." --Elisabeth Kübler-Ross

Death leaves a heartache no one can heal; love leaves a memory no one can steal. – Irish Saying

One flesh. Or if you prefer, one ship. The starboard engine has gone. I, the port engine, must chug along somehow till we make harbour. Or rather, till the journey ends.-- C.S. Lewis, Irish author, literary critic and poet

I'm a much nicer person since my wife died. I found out what pain is, so on that level I'm much nicer. --Hugh Leonard, Irish playwright and author

The Irish have a way with words. I agree with Hugh. Losing Marie made me realize that I should not take my partner for granted. Losing her was painful and it made me a better person.

Tears, of course, are a common theme:

When you are sorrowful look again in your heart, and you shall see that in truth you are weeping for that which has been your delight. – Kahlil Gibran

It's so curious: one can resist tears and 'behave' very well in the hardest hours of grief. But then someone makes you a friendly sign behind a window, or one notices that a flower that was in bud only yesterday has suddenly blossomed, or a letter slips from a drawer… and everything collapses. – Colette

"There is a sacredness in tears. They are not the mark of weakness, but of power. They speak more eloquently than ten thousand tongues. They are the messengers of overwhelming grief, of deep contrition, and of unspeakable love." – Washington Irving

The next three quotes express my feelings about not being able to avoid the grieving process.

While grief is fresh, every attempt to divert only irritates. You must wait till it be digested, and then amusement will dissipate the remains of it. – Samuel Johnson

"Grief is like the ocean; it comes on waves ebbing and flowing. Sometimes the water is calm, and sometimes it is overwhelming. All we can do is learn to swim." – Vicki Harrison

"When someone you love dies, and you're not expecting it, you don't lose her all at once; you lose her in pieces over a long time — the way the mail stops coming, and her scent fades from the pillows and even from the clothes in her closet and drawers. Gradually, you accumulate the parts of her that are gone. Just when the day comes — when there's a particular missing part that overwhelms you with the feeling that she's gone, forever — there comes another day, and another specifically missing part." – John Irving, *A Prayer for Owen Meany*

The death of a dear friend, wife, brother, lover, which seemed nothing but privation, somewhat later assumes the aspect of a guide or genius; for it commonly operates revolutions in our way of life, terminates an epoch of infancy or of youth which was waiting to be closed, breaks up a wonted occupation, or a household, or style of living, and allows the formation of new ones more friendly to the growth of character. -- Ralph Waldo Emerson, American author

Marie's death did shake my foundations. I lost friends and made new ones. I moved 600 miles away. I also learned to value experiences over acquiring stuff.

Even royalty is touched by grief:
"Grief is the price we pay for love." – Queen Elizabeth II

"Believe me, every heart has its secret sorrows, which the world knows not, and oftentimes we call a man cold, when he is only sad." – Henry Wadsworth Longfellow, Hyperion

What happens to us when we die?

"My life closed twice before its close;
It yet remains to see
If Immortality unveil
A third event to me,
So huge, so hopeless to conceive,
As these that twice befell.
Parting is all we know of heaven,
And all we need of hell."   –Emily Dickinson

This is one of my favorite quotes about life after a loss:
"You will lose someone you can't live without, and your heart will be badly broken, and the bad news is that you never completely get over the loss of your beloved. But this is also the good news. They live forever in your broken heart that doesn't seal back up. And you come through. It's like having a broken leg that never heals perfectly – that still hurts when the weather gets cold, but you learn to dance with the limp." – Anne Lamott

Give sorrow words; the grief that does not speak whispers the o'er-fraught heart and bids it break. – William Shakespeare

William, I took your advice and gave my sorrow words. It helped. Thank you.

ACKNOWLEDGMENTS

I rarely agree with Hillary Clinton. However, her statement that "it takes a village to raise a child," is accurate. The same can be said about a book being written. Sure, the author does the writing, but many people contribute.

I wrote much of the book after my relationship with Cynthia began. She is largely responsible for my finding joy in my life after losing Marie. She also tolerated many lonely hours while I was in my office composing and typing. Thank you, Cynthia, I love you.

I would also like to thank my editor, Deirdra Funcheon, for taking my scribblings and turning them into an actual book. She helped me navigate the uncharted waters of e-publishing and made the process very easy. Thank you, Deirdra.

Again using the village metaphor, no one experiences a grief journey alone. My children Kristy and Bradley put their lives on hold to come and care for their mom. I could not have done it without their help. They, of course, experienced the crushing grief of losing their parent. They also had to try to come to terms that their dad was somehow smiling again while they were still grieving. I just want them both to know that I love them both very dearly and am so proud of the amazing people they have become. Thank you, Kristy and Brad.

My friends and church family were a big part of my grief journey. Thank you, St. John's UCC for the meals, the hugs, and the shoulders to cry on. I love all of you.

Marie's sister, Jane, has been my friend since we met 40 years ago. She was by my side throughout Marie's illness and we comforted each other after our spouses died. She has been supportive of my relationship with Cynthia. She was with me every step of my (our) grief journey and I will always treasure her friendship. Thank you, Jane.

Finally, I would love to be able to thank the person without whom this book would not exist, my late wife, Marie. We spent many years together and she will always be a part of who I am. She was always a tough fighter, her toughness never more evident than in her last fight. She kept up the fight long after doctors told her it was over. She also was more worried about me being alone than about her dying. That selfless attitude showed me not how to die, but rather how to live. Thank you, Marie.

ABOUT THE AUTHOR

Dave McClellan grew up in Pennsylvania and is a Penn State diehard through and through. A longtime lumber salesman who switched careers and became a teacher at age 53, he has two children and wrote his first book, *Roses In the Snow*, to cope with the loss of his wife of 40 years, Marie. He now lives in South Carolina.

Marie

Cynthia

Made in the USA
Columbia, SC
10 July 2018